Testimonials

"*By The Big Cedar Tree* reminds us that friendships are often forged through a journey and the pursuit of a common cause. J.W. Embury does a masterful job recounting the adventures of five best friends and the "wild idea" they create in the Oregon wilderness. Little did they know what their idea would come to mean to them and so many others. You won't be able to put this book down!"

Lahn B. Simmons

CRPC - 7 Traits Consultant, Registered Investment Advisor

"From the first page, *By The Big Cedar Tree*, drew me in and I almost immediately felt the power of deep friendship, camaraderie, and teamwork. This is a wonderful testament to abiding friendship, which endured for over 40 years. Even when all the friends went their separate ways and experienced the ups and downs of life, the cabin and what it came to mean to them kept them together and in touch. Not only in touch but truly caring for each other, which extended to the next generation as well. Would that we all could have friends like John and the cabin group. I highly recommend reading."

Deborah Rodney

Book Club Group Leader, Retired Paralegal

"*By the Big Cedar Tree* is J. W. Embury's captivating memoir of his formative years through adulthood. He takes us on a journey through high school where he struggled to secure his identity, make sense of the world at a confusing time, and connect with friends. These issues sorted themselves out on mountain trails, and eventually in shared experiences at a cabin in the woods. This is a story of how a place and being in nature allowed him and others to forge platonic bonds on and off mountains."

Jon Larsen
Esq, World Traveler, Goodreads Champion

A wilderness trip
led to a discovery
that changed their
lives forever

BY THE

BIG CEDAR

TREE

Will their forty-year
old secret be exposed?

By J. W. Embury

Dedicated to Sandy, my true friend, my eternal companion. She knows my heart and how much I value friendships, especially with all those who have made the journey with me passing by the Big Cedar Tree.

"The rain beats down rhythmically on the roof as we pack our final things to prepare for the wet and rainy trek back down to the civilized world. But for these last few minutes, it does still feel like a dream. . .a place in my mind I might go to escape the stress and complexity of life, to find an inner purpose. . .to become a child again. . .

And when I am fully immersed in my life back home, I'll close my eyes and think of this place, and it will emerge in my mind as the perfect magical place in the woods—waiting, always waiting, for someone to walk across its welcoming porch, open the front door, and arrive at the Shangri-La of one's dreams.

For all who have been here, they know. They understand the magic. I believe that's why it's been a closely guarded secret for so many years...shared only amongst discerning and respectful friends. . ."

—JQ

Introduction

O ver forty years ago in a remote part of the Willamette National Forest, two adventuresome young men walked across a cedar bridge that nature created, crossing over a small stream that lead to a tiny clearing, and then farther on to a small nearby lake. These stripling adventurers decided a cabin should be built in that inconsequential clearing, and it was. Soon the cabin welcomed any and all who happened to find it.

Built with old-fashioned tools, the cabin was surrounded by vine maple trees, huckleberry bushes, and rhododendrons. It's a quiet spot, where this unassuming cabin minds its own business. The principal trees in this forest are western hemlock, Douglas fir, and some western red cedar. No real trail leads here; in fact, several hundred yards must be navigated off the nearest trail just to find the Big Cedar Tree, and then another few hundred yards to the cabin—if you know which direction to take. There are no roads to this place and the trail that brings you here climbs several thousand feet in elevation over a four-mile stretch.

🌲

In 2017, Oregon wildfires charred more than 517,000 acres. After the fire, Terry knew full well what drove him to go up the trail; like myself, he just wanted to know if the cabin was still there. He had no way of knowing what to expect or any idea about the damage a major forest fire could do to the landscape and terrain.

Sandy-haired with bright eyes, Terry was fit for a man of sixty-one years. His medium-sized frame was not all sinew and fiber, yet his legs, lungs, and heart were often exercised. He enjoyed taking pictures of the scenic beauty and animals he saw in nature. Most men lacked his tenacity and resolve. He loved being immersed in the outdoors where he would ponder, pray, and seek guidance for those he had the responsibility to help and serve. But right now, he needed to focus his energy on navigating his way safely to the cabin.

The usual access route was closed. Not to be deterred, Tom stealthily bushwhacked around the beginning of the trail in the darkness of the early morning and crossed the road several hundred yards away from the watchful eyes of the guard who sat in a vehicle focused on the trailhead.

He hadn't even traveled a half mile up the trail when the sun began to rise and give light to his surroundings. The scene before him sent chills down his back—the forest fire had burned almost everything right to the ground. Most of the underbrush was torched; bushes and shrubs were all gone. Most of the standing trees were dead, soon to potentially become windfall.

In order to keep hillsides intact, root systems of small bushes, trees, and even mosses and weeds fill in around the rocks and soil. This undergrowth holds everything together like netting beneath the ground. In the area surrounding the cabin, the forest fire burned up all that netting and entire hillsides lost their footing, causing many places to fall apart and slide downhill along parts of the trail. There were dirt slides, rockslides, gravel slides, logs rolling and tumbling. In some places-big rocks were impaled into the bark of trees. How hard would you have to throw a rock at a tree for it to stick?

Probably a third of the trail wasn't recognizable at all—it was just gone. Huge avalanches of rock and dirt covered the trail in many places. There might be a rock the size of a tank or semi-truck where the trail had been. Even finding the trail was impossible at times, but Terry always knew where he was going. As he walked and crawled across unstable taluses, they would slip out from underneath him to restart some small landslides. He was actually afraid he was going to be swallowed up by the small avalanches he was creating.

At certain points Terry walked across a thick carpet of bright orange pine needles that had burned off the trees and floated to the ground. His hiking became quiet. Walking through the area was almost mystical—it left him in awe. The thick lushness of the carpet deadened the sound of his footsteps. There were no sounds of birds, no bugs, no buzzing noises. Nothing. Terry thought, *Where had they all gone? How many were consumed by the fire? When would those beautiful sounds return?*

The fire was still burning in a number of areas with pretty heavy smoke in the air and occasional isolated tree fires. At times, Terry crawled on all fours and zigzagged to try to find a good route because the trail was nonexistent. He realized again how dangerous this journey was. As he looked farther up the canyon, hoping, ever hoping, he wondered if the Lunch Tree had survived. Shocked, he saw a couple other big trees had fallen right next to it, but Rob's favorite tree was fine.

As he went through the Cedar Grove, he started to encounter things still aflame. Several trees were burning. One big, hollow log looked like it had a furnace inside. As he continued farther up the trail and "turned the corner," there were still charred trees burning amid unaffected areas. This mosaic pattern that the fire had taken gave him a measure of hope about the cabin as he pressed forward.

For over five hours Terry had been struggling to get through nature's inferno just to reach the jump-off point. That spot was not even recognizable, but he knew where to go. Of course he did; he'd traveled this trail hundreds of times over the past thirty years.

The last landmark, the Big Cedar Tree, would soon be within sight. Had the fire consumed the Big Cedar? The air was filled with a lot of smoke, making it difficult to see very far. More trees were burning as he approached the small grove where the Big Cedar tree had stood as a sentinel, the sentinel we'd used for so many decades to navigate to the cabin. It takes six or seven people's outstretched arms and clasped hands to circle the Big Cedar. Whenever I hiked past that magnificent tree I would always reach out and touch it before I continued onward toward the cabin. It was my way of expressing my gratitude and respect. Miraculously, Terry discovered the Big Cedar standing mostly unscarred with the fire burning nearby.

He made his way toward the cabin, knowing that soon his long journey would be over. He was still too far away to discover what he desperately wanted to know, so he quickened his pace. Then, he discovered there was no need to rush onward—he stopped abruptly, looking at the reality before him.

Chapter 1
Survived

"The clearest way into the Universe is through a forest wilderness," —John Muir

1971

Rob and I stepped over the guardrail and began walking as the sunrise made shadows of our two figures. The shadows looked odd, like hunchbacks.

I was wearing a yellow hooded track sweatshirt, no pants—I only had on my old-fashioned long john underwear. My jeans were stuffed away in my pack, too wet to wear. Rob had on a flannel shirt and a pair of jeans, and he was carrying a double-bladed axe. His shadow looked even stranger than mine.

The highway noise from the cars and trucks rushing past us was almost deafening compared to the silence we had been immersed in for five days. We walked more than a mile before we came to a long gravel driveway where a small house was almost completely hidden by the surrounding trees. Had it not been wintertime, the house would have been nearly impossible to see.

Seeing smoke coming out of the chimney, we discussed and even rehearsed what we would do as we approached the house. Choosing the back door to announce our arrival, Rob knocked. A woman came to the door and opened it just far enough to peer out. With only one eye visible and some grayish-brown hair peeking from behind the door, she assessed the situation.

We could smell bacon frying and other pleasant breakfast aromas. I suspected the food was about ready to eat. There was warmth in that house. My hunger and near-hypothermic body condition almost took over and propelled me to barge right past the woman, but I stayed where I was.

Rob asked if we could use the phone with his trademark congenial smile. Her voice was soft but blunt; without much hesitation, she said, "Sorry don't have a phone; there's one down the road at the tavern. Abruptly, her one eye disappeared as the door quickly closed, leaving us both dumbfounded.

I looked at Rob and asked, "Clearly we must have scared her?" Neither of us had bathed in over five days and we looked like two young homeless guys looking for a handout. Rob's mostly blondish brown hair was matted and in desperate need of some shampoo. I, too, needed lots of soap. Edgy, anxious, and perplexed, we turned and walked farther down the road for another half mile, maybe more. We approached a building with a couple cars parked out front. After offloading our backpacks, we climbed the three steps to the door and walked inside.

When we entered the warm old building, we encountered a bunch of old guys playing billiards and having a few beers. I wouldn't call it a tavern, nor a bar. It just seemed like a gathering place for the locals. Thankfully, it had a phone we could use. The first thing Rob did was to call home and let his mom know we were okay. It had been five days since anyone had heard from us. Jean, his mother, was always calm and collected. She never got mad or raised her voice. She commented, "Well, we were starting to worry about you and were thinking about calling search and rescue," and within about an hour and a half, she was there to pick us up.

Back at Rob's place, we evaluated our situation. We were tired, hungry, and seriously dirty. Minutes after arriving, I headed down to the basement shower. The warm water hurt because I had a mild case of frostbite in my feet. Despite the pain, I stood in that shower for what seemed like a half hour. Finally I got out, got dressed, and tried to reflect upon the whole experience. It was incredible—astonishing, in a lot of ways, that we had even survived. If either one of us had even so much as sprained an ankle, it would have been bad.

FIVE DAYS THAT CHANGED MY LIFE

Day 1

When we left Rob's home, it was raining hard. There would be snow at higher elevations. As we traveled and neared our drop-off point, I thought, *Why did I agree to do this and leave behind the warmth of Rob's house?* The weather forecast suggested it would only get colder over the next few days. As we neared the dam that provided electricity to a community near where we lived, played, and had grown up, my sense of adventure returned.

For years, I had wanted to know where those power lines went. The swath of land they traveled through was enormous, a wilderness that very few had access to. What secrets were up there? What discoveries could we make, and were there any cabins or remote lakes to be found?

Our quasi-plan was to travel until the gravel road ended, then cross the large creek that fed into the river. At that point we would follow the power lines until we reached the summit and discovered who knows what?

▲

Usually we would drive a 1953 Chevy Suburban on our various outings, but this time, Rob's parents hadn't wanted us to leave the "Green Machine" (as I liked to call it) alongside a busy road for three days. Thus, we needed someone to drive us the forty-plus miles to the starting point for our semi-planned adventure. After no real luck asking the usual friends and family, I convinced Kathy, a high school classmate, to drive us.

Kathy was super popular and great looking. Her dark brown hair shaped her face beautifully, and her soft brown eyes seemed to peer into my soul and see right through me. For most of my senior year in high school, I tried everything to convince Kathy to like me as more than just a friend. She was content to stay with her boyfriend. She knew I'd dated lots of girls in high school and I fancied myself as a charmer, but she would have none of my predicable seductions.

🔱

We arrived at the road several miles away from the dam, but Kathy did not want to drive her parents' car on the gravel. Therefore she abruptly dropped us off at the beginning of the gravel road that led to our intended starting point. We didn't really know how far we would need to walk before we could begin our adventure, but thought that Kathy would have driven us farther. Oh well.

As we took our packs out of the trunk, Kathy commented that the weather was going to get worse and to be careful. These were great words of encouragement from someone sitting in a warm car who would soon be back home to take in the New Year with family and friends. We thanked her and gave no indication that the next several unplanned miles of hiking would even faze us. As we watched her drive away I thought, *What have I gotten myself into?*

We had walked maybe a half mile before I remarked to Rob, "I wished she'd driven us to the trailhead. This road is just wet and muddy." Stoic and determined to stay positive, Rob only responded with a rhetorical question, "Whining already?"

Our view was limited because the densely forested mountains rose so rapidly from the river. If there was snow ahead of us, we wouldn't know about it for quite some time—and how deep that snow would be, we had no idea. Rob acted like the snow wouldn't be an issue for our adventure. He possesses a unique quality of conveying optimism with his very calm, quiet, and confident demeanor. Having gone on many adventures with him, I'd come to know his optimism was compelling, but all too often lacked realism about what lay ahead of us. Or perhaps he just lived so much in the moment that any possible negative consequences were simply never considered seriously.

The weight of my pack reflected a measure of good planning on my part, yet something inside me said I should've brought snowshoes for both of us. Wet and weary, we finally reached the end of the road—marked by a rushing, roaring creek that stood in the way of the next phase of our adventure. The power lines on the other side led upward, away from civilization.

The rain hadn't abated and nightfall was coming fast, so we called it a day. "Rob, how are we going to stay dry in all this rain?"

Confidently, he answered, "Let's locate a spot that slightly slopes downhill and make small trenches to divert the water. Should be pretty simple." We combined tarps and made our shelter, but true to form, it rained throughout the night. Water crept into my space, and the bottom part of my sleeping bag became damp. This did not bode well.

Day 2

Our breakfast consisted of peanut butter and jelly sandwiches. I had cut some Tillamook cheese slices that I raided from the refrigerator at Rob's house, and we ate those too. Our small morning meal complete, we made ready to cross the creek and continue our adventure.

The prior day we had been paralleling the power lines. Now, the power lines took off steeply up the mountainside. There was no jeep track or trail to be seen. Everywhere we looked was all overgrown with thick brush and small fir trees ranging from five to ten feet tall.

Before we could tackle the mountainside before us, there was the raging creek to contend with—too wide to toss our packs over and too fast to ford unless we wanted to strip down to our underwear and balance our packs above our heads like Sherpas. We discussed that option for less than thirty seconds, and in short order, hiked upstream and found a large log we could walk across. Thank goodness for windfall.

I could see three power line poles, which I used as a visual reference to make a mental distance calculation. They looked about

250 yards apart from one another, shaped like 150-foot tall Saguaro cacti. The goal was simple: Reach one, rest for a bit. Reach another, do the same. We both agreed that we could hike past four or five electric Saguaro cacti well before dark.

Off we went and the next thing I knew, we were hiking in snow. I felt like a human mountain goat carrying a fifty-pound pack. Plodding up the mountainside of brush and trees became a personal ordeal. Soon, mental demons began whispering negative thoughts in my mind. I started to wonder, *Why am I doing this? Am I being punished for my lustful thoughts about Kathy, and instead of ceaselessly rolling a rock to the top of a mountain like Sisyphus, I am to wade in snow up to my crotch forever?*

Rob's adventures often start out seeming like fun, and then become an unplanned test of physical and mental toughness. The first power line pole seemed like it was 400 yards farther up the mountainside. In the summer, I would be able to reach that first pole in fifteen minutes or less; at the rate we were hiking, it would take hours to reach our imagined goal for today's venture. Now, the mountainside sloped up and away so dramatically that only two power line poles could be seen at a time.

Soon Rob and I became separated from each other. He was off to my left about fifty yards and was farther up the mountainside than me—surely because my pack was twenty-five pounds heavier than his. After what seemed like two hours of swimming through snow and brush, we finally passed the first pole. Rob continued nearer the taller trees. He, too, looked to be struggling without making much progress. I was kicking steps in the snow and making crude switchback patterns. I'd stomp steps five or ten feet to my left, and then do the same to my right. Soon, I shed my coat and tied it on the outside of my pack. I wished I had brought ski poles or a long stick. Painstakingly, I made my way clear of the open brush area and got over near the taller trees like Rob had done.

As we passed the second power line pole we rested long enough to eat a sandwich and drink some water. Not having a watch, and with the cloudy sky hiding the sun, I wasn't sure of the time. We finally reached the third pole late in the day. We were exhausted from slogging through the snow for six-plus hours. Running out of daylight, we decided to make shelter about ten yards to the left of the pole where two nice fifteen-foot Christmas trees stood. As darkness closed in on us, the cloud cover was disappearing and the temperature was dropping considerably. What seemed like a 35-degree daytime high was turning into a 20-degree night with the wind chill.

After scanning the site, Rob smiled and commented, "John, let's cut some fir boughs from these young trees. They'll keep us off the snow and make great mattresses."

My flannel shirt was wet, as were my pants. Too exhausted to say much, I just replied, "That sounds good—I'm getting cold."

I laid my tarp out so that if it snowed during the night I'd stay reasonably dry. That done, I laid out my sleeping bag on the fir boughs, tore off my clothes, and hung them inside out on some branches of the adjacent fir tree, including my socks. My pack was conveniently propped within reach for things like food, water, and my meager supply of remaining dry clothes. That accomplished, I jumped into my sleeping bag to get warm. I looked over at Rob and saw a little smirk on his face. I was too tired to care. My only intent was to avoid exiting my sleeping bag until sunrise or later.

Rob was wiser in his methods. He used his tarp for cover as I did. He carefully took his wet clothes off and placed them on the fir boughs, then placed his sleeping bag on top of them. Then he crawled into his sleeping bag, making strange moaning sounds—of joy, I hope. Before long, he was asleep and snoring like a hibernating bear.

Hunger got in the way of sleep. I reached in my pack and opened up a can of Dinty Moore Stew. I inhaled it in mere minutes. My stomach somewhat satisfied, I put a stocking hat on and buried myself into my sleeping bag, determined to create warmth. I soon drifted into a deep sleep.

I awoke to the sound of wind causing my tarp to groan. As I tried to secure my tarp from becoming a flag flapping in the wind, I looked out to see celestial lights glimmering above me. No light pollution from human sources dimmed my view, and I briefly found myself in awe of those divinely created constellations. The night sky was completely cloudless. That night there was no New Year's Eve celebration for Rob and me, watching TV where thousands of people in New York City would be celebrating with Dick Clark as he announced the falling of a symbolic ball from atop a building at Times Square to usher in the New Year. Instead, my 1971 New Year celebration was filled with wonder at my surroundings.

Day 3

We awoke to more cold and clear blue skies. The problem before me was simple but also challenging: My only clothes for hiking, hanging from the limbs of a small Christmas tree, were stiff and mostly frozen. Rob's clothes were dry, and he was already dressed and ready to continue our adventure. My Levis were nearly impossible to put on. I had to whack them against the same tree they had hung from overnight. With considerable effort, they became pliable enough to slip over my legs. They were cold and wet, making my long johns feel damp. My nice wool socks were inside out, and they, too, needed pounding against a tree limb to become pliable enough to pull on my feet.

Rob had that same smirk on his face from last night, and he knew I had just gone to great pains to get dressed. I was not in the mood to discuss my folly and, fortunately for him, he just kept quiet. We packed up quickly with the plan to reach some summit somewhere so that we could overlook where we had come and hopefully see the river below.

Day three was no different than the previous. More brush, more wading in waist-deep snow, with the addition of a cold wind now blowing at our backs from the canyon below. I was more miserable than the day before. Again, Rob and I separated from each other as we each made our way up the mountainside. Doing so eliminated the aid of friends encouraging one another onward. Alone, I came to doubt that I possessed the inner strength to reach our next stopping point for the night. Minutes seemed like hours. No friendly banter occurred that day. I was left alone with my own thoughts and self-doubt.

Late in the day, I spotted a head of unmistakable blond hair trudging along ahead of me. Rob was a considerable distance away from the power lines, on the edge of the dense forest. He looked spent but glanced my way. Seeing him so close was motivation to press onward. I angled my way toward him, moving closer to where I might catch up to him. Finally, after several hours had passed, we spoke to each other. I was relieved to find him in good spirits and not suffering from exhaustion or worse, hypothermia. I was cold, very tired, and hungry. We took stock of our surroundings and continued trudging forward to where the power lines seemed to be leveling off.

It seemed that we had finally attained our goal of reaching the power lines' peak. I felt a sense of triumph, but our mission had been exhausting. "Rob, I'm done in. I think we need to get a fire started and talk about heading back to the highway, but definitely not the way we came."

"Why not the way we came?"

"Well, I'm not going to retrace my footsteps down that slope. I say we head down this other watershed first thing tomorrow morning."

"We don't even know what that hiking will be like. It could be a lot worse, actually."

I was so exhausted and cold that everything I seemed to be doing felt like I was in slow motion. There was no further talk of heading back the way we had traveled for the past three days. Hiking a little farther on, we reached the top of where we thought the watershed/canyon began, and Rob finally put the axe he brought to good use by felling a small tree.

We limbed the tree's fir boughs and made a huge, king-size bed at least two feet thick. I worked on getting our tarps situated for a peaceful night's sleep. Rob had begun building a fire from the fallen tree, which was an exercise in futility because the tree was not dead. The wood was green. Using it to start a fire was nearly impossible. After considerable amount of time, we found dry firewood. Nightfall was rapidly approaching and after lots of matches and quite a bit of effort, a good-sized fire began to warm us up. I desperately needed that warmth. Talking was sparse, as we both were completely focused on getting warm. Soon fatigue took its hold on us and we called it a night. Once again the sky was celestial and our view of the heavens above was grand. As I gazed northward I glimpsed the aurora borealis as it swept across the sky ever so briefly. I continued to search the sky to marvel at the pink, green, yellow, blue, and violet lights, but instead I saw some shooting stars and finally drifted off to the sound of Rob's bear-like snoring.

Day 4

We awoke ready to get going. We stashed some clothes, cooking pans, and other supplies in a cache until we could return at a later date. We were determined to reach the highway, several miles below us, before dark. As we set out, we trekked through an old-growth forest that had probably never been logged and hadn't seen a major forest fire in nearly a hundred years. Surprisingly, the terrain sloped gradually downhill. There was very little brush and not much windfall. The snow depth was less than a foot. Soon, we were out of the snow and at the headwaters of a small creek. Reaching the summit of the power line poles was our initial goal, and I was giddy knowing that we were now heading downhill and eventually back home to civilization. I remarked to Rob, "I'm so glad to be out of the snow. What do you say we bust out that can of Lady Alberta peaches to celebrate having made it to the summit of the power lines? There were a couple times I wondered if we should have turned back, did you?"

Rather than answering my question, Rob asked, "You have the peaches in your pack, right?"

I offloaded my pack and quickly found the can. "Here, put your pocketknife to good use and open up the can. I've waited four days for this treat. I was tempted to break out this can of peaches on New Years Eve, but I was too damn tired."

Rob stabbed the first peach half with his knife, entirely devouring it, and just as quickly exclaimed, "Lady Alberta peaches are the best, don't you think so?" With the lid removed he showed me the three remaining large peach halves, which were surrounded by sweet peach juice. I was more than ready to celebrate. We each took turns eating our peach halves and taking long gulps of the juice in the can. I slurped the last of the peach juice and agreed, "Rob, Lady Alberta peaches are the food of the gods."

We promised each other that we would return the next summer to this very spot. Before heading onward, Rob wedged the empty peach can between the trunk of a tree and one of its limbs, thinking we would be able to see the peach can from a distance upon our return.

Trekking onward, we quickly passed through this special open area where fir, cedar, and western hemlock trees stood as sentinels. The morning breeze that touched our faces was cool, not cold. As I gazed all around, I found myself filled with a feeling of respect and reverence.

How hard could it be to walk downhill four or five miles following a beautiful creek? The creek carved its way down the canyon, creating a steeper stream that was difficult to walk along. We started out paralleling the creek about thirty yards above its shoreline. Soon, the open forest gave way to denser vegetation and the creek continued to slope steadily downward. We discovered some waterfalls that required traversing; each time we did so, we ended up farther above the creek bottom.

We were growing tired and hungry. Our pace was slowed due to the steep canyon and our constant bushwhacking. We forgot about the time and how quickly we were running out of daylight, but gradually began to hear the sounds of semitrucks as they drove past where the canyon opened up and reached the highway.

The recurring rumbling of engines that represented the end of our ordeal drove me forward. With civilization imminent, we surely were close to an area where we could find a house with a phone to call someone who would come to our rescue. As we pressed farther downward, our traversing put us about 400 feet above the creek bottom. In my impatience, I threw caution to the wind and became laser-focused on leading us out of this long-forgotten beautiful canyon and creek before dark.

Rob had begun to slow his pace and was no longer keeping up. Our traversing was exhausting, and as I looked down at the creek I realized how much easier it would be to walk along the creek bottom. I could do a form of glissading to take me very quickly down to the creek's edge. "Rob, watch this." All I had to do was simply hop, jump, and lean back on my backpack to propel me down to the creek.

Surprisingly, I made it to the bottom quickly without getting skewered, breaking any of my limbs, or smashing into a tree or rocks. When I reached the bottom I was quite proud of myself, and before looking back toward where I'd come, I said, "You've got to try this Rob, it's a great way to get down the hill!" I thought Rob might have followed my lead.

Not so—he just hollered, "John, that was an insane thing to do," and despite my shouting encouragement from the edge of the creek, Rob refused to use my method to join me. I ended up waiting at least fifteen minutes as he sauntered his way to the creek bottom.

Unfortunately, the creek continued to drop steeply downward, forcing us to go back up along the mountainside around both a small and large waterfall. The forest was growing darker, and daylight was vanishing. Yet, the sounds of the highway grew louder and louder. Those sounds were driving us to ignore the impending darkness as we pressed forward with reckless abandon.

I led, with Rob close by. The sound of semitrucks was becoming my noise beacon, like a foghorn used to warn mariners as they approached landfall, helping them to look for a safe entry into a harbor. I simply kept walking onward around trees and bushes, thinking that any moment we'd be at the highway.

Suddenly, I noticed I could only see about four or five feet ahead in the dark. I had the sense that I was becoming careless and not evaluating my surroundings very wisely. In the next instant, as I reached up and grabbed some branches of a large bush impeding my progress, my right leg reached out to find secure footing, but encountered nothing but air.

Quickly I hollered to Rob, "STOP AND CLIMB UP HILL." I did the same, scrambling on all fours straight uphill about fifty to seventy-five feet back the way we had just come. Off to my left about twenty feet from me was Rob. We both knew it was too dark to continue, and neither of us knew if we were near a cliff or not. "Rob, I'm not going any farther down the canyon tonight." Going forward was unacceptable. We each looked around for a place to sleep. Just a few feet away, I could make out two trees growing close enough together that I could wedge myself safely between them. Rob found a spot to roll out his sleeping bag and asked, "Do you hear the sounds of the cars and trucks in the distance?"

"Yeah, why?"

"Well, that noise seems loud to me, the highway must be very close."

"I sure hope so."

I removed my pack and placed it on the uphill side of one of the trees and hauled out my damp sleeping bag. Rob rolled his sleeping bag out on a slight slope, where the bottom of the bag was up against some small bushes. Neither of us was inclined to talk much more.

I searched in my pack for some food and found a can of soup. I took my pocketknife and crudely opened the top of the can, ate-drank cold soup, and settled in for a long night. I was exhausted and in need of food and warmth, very disappointed that we hadn't reached the highway. The darkness hung heavy and the weather, though warmer than the night before, still hovered around freezing. My flannel sleeping bag was bulky, heavy, and damp around my feet.

The last dry clothes I had were my yellow track sweats. I put those on and stuffed my wet clothes into the bottom of my pack. Positioned almost as if I was sitting in a chair, I looked out into the darkness and tried to drift off to sleep. "Goodnight, Rob." Instead of a reply, all I heard was his usual deep snoring. I didn't mind.

Two things plagued me the entire night. Firstly, I couldn't get warm. Instead of drifting off into sleep I drifted into periods of shivering and shuddering. Secondly, when I looked over to where Rob was lying, I noticed his dark shape had started slipping down the hillside. Concerned, I would yell at him from time to time, demanding that he move up the slope. He would mumble back at me and then scoot up the hillside a bit.

This went on for most of the night. Between shivering and annoying Rob about slipping down the hill, I continued to hear the sound of trucks going by on the highway. The sound seemed so very close, almost too loud. Oh, how I wanted to sleep. I just wanted to sleep all cozy and warm. Several times I was tempted to get out of my sleeping bag, jump up and down, stomp my feet, and get some blood circulating. Instead, I just sat in between those two trees and shivered. I couldn't wait for daylight. This adventure was wearing on my nerves and all I wanted to do was get the heck out of the mountains and back to civilization.

Day 5

When it became light enough to see I pulled my boots back on and stuffed my sleeping bag in my backpack, hollering at Rob to get up and get going. His reply was classic Rob: "What's the rush, John, you have some place you need to be?"

Damn right I do, I thought. *You originally told me we'd be gone for two nights, three at the most.* To our surprise, we discovered we'd slept that night near the edge of a cliff, surrounded on three sides where it dropped off thirty to fifty feet. Wedged between those two trees, I was actually very near the cliff's edge. Rob was less than three feet from where the cliff dropped off.

As we traversed down to the creek bottom, the highway noises grew even louder, and I believed we were less than half mile from some form of self-rescue. Soon enough, we found ourselves busting through the brush and out to the edge of the highway. Looking back, I could have easily fallen to my death or been seriously injured had I not stopped myself the night before when I started to step out into the "thin air." Clearly, Providence had been watching over us, and we stepped over the guardrail and began walking toward civilization.

Chapter 2
Found the Cache

"The farther one gets into the wilderness, the greater is the attraction of its lonely freedom." —Theodore Roosevelt

Rob and I met in 1967 during our sophomore year of high school. I was new to town, having recently moved from a smaller rural area to live with my father and stepmother after my mother suffered a severe mental breakdown. This was a very difficult time for me; my world had been turned upside down.

After my parents' divorce, I didn't see my dad that much until my mother was no longer able to care for my three younger siblings and myself and he was compelled to take custody of us. That was a big transition for everyone. After a few months, we started to settle into our new family structure. I didn't particularly like the routine, but my father and stepmother didn't seem to care if I came home after school for dinner or if I spent time elsewhere. I chose elsewhere as often as possible.

I knew Rob because he was involved in cross country and track, and very popular. He was a rising star in the Oregon track and field world. Rob's quiet demeanor and inner self-confidence were void of any conceit, boasting, or vaunting, but his dry sense of humor became obvious as soon as you started talking with him. He was a natural athlete, very bright, and excelled academically as well. Rob was never considered a jock. He was considered a runner. Many girls in high school would pursue him rather than wait to be pursued.

As a high school freshman I, too, had competed in track and field, but I was not a runner like Rob. My events were far less glamorous: the high jump, long jump, and triple jump. During this sophomore year at my new school, I was determined to make the varsity squad.

At this school everyone was required to take a physical education class, and in the spring, our school's physical education depart-
ment hosted a five-event track competition with mandatory participation. I knew that this competition was my chance to do well and
make an impression on the track coaches, who didn't know much
about me. After competing to the best of my ability (and winning
more points than Rob), not only did I later make the varsity track
team, but Rob and I also became friends. Our friendship developed
to the point where we were not only teammates, but also did other
things together. Hiking and camping became something we would
do frequently.

Rob grew up having camping and hunting experiences, especially with his father and his dad's close friend. During deer and elk
hunting season, they often traveled to eastern Oregon to a favorite
spot they called Indian Rock. In my youth, my father went deer or
elk hunting too, but I was only taken once.

Because of Rob's outdoor experience, he developed excellent
camping skills. He seemed to understand the importance of our national forests and the natural wildlife it contains. I witnessed firsthand the great joy and satisfaction Rob enjoyed out in the elements.
Whenever we went on some camping excursion or adventure, I had
the opportunity to learn and discover up close what being out in
nature was all about.

The year 1968 was filled with sadness and insanity. The music
of neither The Beatles nor The Rolling Stones could drown out
most Americans' sorrow regarding the tragic assassinations of
Martin Luther King, Jr. and Senator Robert F. Kennedy. At that
time, I didn't know enough about them—their personal and politi-
cal histories—to really grasp the significance of their deaths, but it
still bothered me. Even if I didn't understand the circumstances, I
knew that killing innocent people was wrong. By the time the year
ended, I came to realize that their deaths left most Americans ques-
tioning many things about our societal values and the responsibility
we had to each other and a nation. I certainly did.

Living with my father and stepmother became increasingly difficult to deal with, mostly because my father was an alcoholic and it

would be decades before he would eventually go into recovery. As a result, I found myself spending a lot more time at Rob's house. It was significantly more pleasant than my dad's. At Rob's home, his family was welcoming and his mother was especially kind and friendly. She was engaged in and supportive of her children's lives. There were always projects and chores to be done around Rob's place. Because I was able to help with some of the chores from time to time, I was welcomed at the family dinner table—but even if there were no chores, I was always included. Having some chores to do made me feel like less of a freeloader and more worthy of eating there on a regular basis. I conveniently found myself spending the night at Rob's house often. It was a little weird at first, but eventually I just blended in and his parents didn't seem to mind—at least, no one ever asked me to go home. Rob never made a big deal about me frequently spending the night. He just seemed to understand that I didn't want to go home to my dysfunctional family life three miles down the road.

Rob generally hung out with the varsity runners when he wasn't involved in academics. Unlike Rob, I wasn't much involved in academics or student government. However, I was very involved in track and befriending cute girls.

One of the varsity runners Rob trained with was named Dave. He was in his senior year in 1968. Dave had moved from California to our small Willamette river town a few years earlier. He was very introverted, but hardworking and talented. Personally, I found Dave a bit intimidating. Perhaps this was because he seemed so self-confident and self-assured. Pure rugged muscle, he probably had to shave twice daily. He acted more mature than us—actually, upon reflection, Dave just was more mature than us.

Rob and Dave ran similar distances. They both specialized in the 880-yard race and the mile run. Dave had become an elite runner in the state of Oregon, and Rob was well on his way. In high school they both competed against formidable opponents like Steve Prefontaine and others, becoming close friends in the process. Upon high school graduation in 1968, Dave attended college in Oregon.

⚜

On April 25, 1969, Rob and I went to the Corvallis Invitational to watch Steve Prefontaine, the reigning mile and two-mile state champion, run against Dave Crooks, who had run a national best of 9:01 earlier in the year. Steve, who had started to gain widespread attention, was called "Pre" by his devoted fans. He possessed raw determination and a unique running style that would become his trademark: breaking first, running from the front, and keeping the competition at his heels with what appeared to be his sheer force of will. We had the best "seats" in the stadium, leaning against the railing at the finish line that kept spectators off the track. For over an hour, we'd held our spots. There was a skiff of breeze and the temperature seemed to be about 55 degrees. Neither of these elements would affect the race; if anything, the weather was perfect for running.

We anxiously awaited the final call for the 2-mile run. Pre began his preparations, and when I caught sight of him doing wind sprints on the infield, I asked Rob how many wind sprints he had previously done. Rob's comment was straight to the point: "I'm not sure, but Pre has been running back and forth for about twenty minutes." My own legs began to ache as I thought of what twenty minutes of wind sprints would do to me. Growing more impatient, I only cared to hear the final call for the 2-mile.

Finally, the announcement came. "Final call for the 2-mile run. All runners report to the official's table, last call, 2-mile run. Ladies and gentlemen, the final event to this year's Corvallis invitational is about to begin. We're pleased to introduce this year's participants for the 2-mile run." A roar from the crowd exploded at the announcement. The applause continued to grow as runners were individually announced. "From Milwaukie High School, with a previous best time of 9:11, Mike Hiefield, and last year's state 2-mile champion with the time of 9:03, Steve Prefontaine. With identical times of 9:01, Dave Crooks from Centennial High School, and Mike Hahn from Benson Tech."

While the announcements took place, Pre had been pacing back and forth no more than ten feet from where we stood. I noticed he was talking to himself and mouthing some words, and as the applause died down I asked Rob, "What is Pre saying?"

Rob yelled back, "He looks to be saying the words, 9:01, 9:01." Suddenly, the race starter said to the runners, "Runners, to your mark, set..." *Bang* went the starter's gun, and the runners were off.

Pre took the lead before reaching the end of the first turn. The pace seemed quick. Rob commented, "Looks like Pre is out for blood; seems to be running a 66-second pace per lap." As Pre completed the first lap, an official called out the time of 67 seconds. With the public announcement of Pre's second lap time, people began to crowd around for a better view of the race. The prospect of a record-breaking time seemed to hang in the air as the anticipation grew.

Several people seemed to be coveting our perfect spot. When the announcer yelled, "Steve Prefontaine leads with a time of 3:20," (after three laps) more people began to push their way toward the finish line. We were being squeezed and jostled from three sides. As people crowded closer to us, I began to imagine how the New York City subway riders must feel during their evening commute home. Yet, as the news of Pre's mile split was announced, I completely forgot my discomfort. "At the mile mark, Prefontaine leads with the time of 4:25." The crowd's roar of excitement and approval seemed to shake the grandstand.

It was obvious that many of the spectators knew a great deal about track and field and felt confident that we were witnessing the unfolding of a great achievement. Though I was standing right next to Rob, I had to yell as loud as I could in order for him to hear me. "How long can Pre keep this up?"

His faint reply was, "Probably until the race is over."

The official split time of the fifth lap was 65 seconds, and I tried to comprehend the true significance of the entire event. I was swept up in the emotion of the crowd and what was taking place before my eyes. All I could see was a young man running as fast as he could; all I could hear was people screaming, "Go Pre, go Pre." When the gun (final) lap sounded, Pre was in an all-out sprint for the entire last lap of the race. As Pre pressed toward the finish line, I yelled again to Rob, but the shouting crowd drowned out my words. As he crossed the finish line, Pre's goal was achieved. My heart pounded like a drum. I, too, cheered at the top of my lungs along with the thousands of other witnesses and said to myself, "He did it!"

I tried to put the race into perspective, knowing that the Oregon State high school 1-mile record was 4:10. Pre had run only six seconds slower than that record. Despite having never run better than a 9:01, Pre ran the first mile in 4:25 and then proceeded to run the second mile in 4:16.5 seconds. His time was 8:41.5!

When I accepted Rob's invitation to attend the Corvallis Invitational, I did so with little-to-no thought that anything of significance was going to happen. It was simply a good excuse to go somewhere and be with my friend Rob. Instead, I witnessed the national high school 2-mile record being broken by several seconds on that April night in 1969. The drama that unfolded before my eyes was neither Shakespearean nor a movie portraying something from the past. Nothing scripted, nothing rehearsed. Witnessing Steve Prefontaine do something remarkable reshaped my view of athletic achievement. The palpable energy there captivated me, and the raw determination of the runners, especially Pre's, resonated with perhaps thousands. Rob had introduced me into his world of high energy and excitement—a runner's world. After enrolling at University of Oregon, where he began running on the national stage, Pre became a true running legend. His running records of achievement are mind-boggling. He competed in the '72 Olympic Trials in Eugene, Oregon. At that time Pre had already won twenty-one college meets in a row. Some students at University of Oregon, inspired by his dominance and the popularity of "Go Pre" t-shirts worn by his fans, created a one-of-a-kind "Stop Pre" t-shirt as a tongue-in-cheek acknowledgement of the impossible. That shirt became synonymous with the legend of Pre himself when he wore it for his victory lap after crushing the competition.

Rob and I continued to do more and more things together, and perhaps it was because I was so interested in his world that our friendship grew. I'd never been around someone as interesting and unique as Rob. I kind of idolized him. Who wouldn't? He would become our high school student body president. His SAT scores enabled him to attend any college of his choice. Not afforded any special treatment or help, he earned everything he achieved in high school. He was modest about his accomplishments. He had no enemies. He was a quiet inspiration to many people, especially me. I knew he liked me and accepted me for who I was. I like to think we were brothers who happened to have completely different biological parents.

🔺

Summer 1971
After Rob and I had recovered from our New Year's adventure tracking the power lines, the decision was made that we would go back, fetch our cached belongings, and do some additional exploring. This time we chose summer to make the trek and actually took a slightly different route than we had in the winter of 1970–71.

It made an amazing difference to hike in the summertime, as compared to our winter snow-wading. What had seemed an impossible climb became a leisurely stroll through a lush, green forest. We were able to locate our peach can and the cache within a few hours. We gathered up our stashed items, tossed them into our almost-empty backpacks, and proceeded to take an entirely different route forward—bushwhacking in search of a trail we anticipated we'd cross in about a mile.

On this route, we encountered dozens of wild rhododendrons with beautiful blooms as they bathed themselves in the cool cover of the dense forest canopy. Wild huckleberry bushes were abundant. Black bears would feast on the ripe huckleberries in another month or so. This wilderness was filled with some grand and majestic groves of trees. Other than the redwood forest in Northern California, I have never seen so many huge cedar trees. In some areas the cedars grouped themselves in several smaller groves. Some of the tree trunks were at least eight to ten feet in diameter.

Because this area of the forest was so dense, many trees had blown down during severe windstorms. Not just cedar trees were blown down, but many Douglas firs as well as Ponderosa Pine. I wonder what windstorm might have caused some of this windfall? Nature has a way of both solving and causing problems. When I was hiking and stopped from time to time to gaze upon the vast wilderness and old growth cedar trees, I pondered what this place would look like in fifty years.

Interestingly, among some northwest coastal American Indian cultures, the western red cedar is often given the names "tree of life" and "life giver." Some tribes called themselves "People of the Cedar." Groves of ancient cedars were symbols of power and gathering places for ceremonies, retreat, and contemplation.[3] I agree completely.

This new, enormous area of forest and nature filled our minds with all sorts of wilderness adventure possibilities. In the late afternoon, we came across the trail we were seeking. It was barely visible due to lack of use; one might have thought it was a game trail. We weren't sure how far we were from the trailhead. Because we were running out of daylight, we decided to jog back as much as we could to make sure we got back before dark. Despite our hurry, we knew we would return to this sacred place.

Chapter 3
Trail Exploration

"Not all who wander are lost." —*J. R. R. Tolkien*

During my junior year of high school I met Mike. He, along with Rob, was part of a group of students who were, as I called them, the "intellectuals"—the ones who were really striving to learn something in high school and make something of themselves after they graduated. I gravitated toward those people because they were interesting and they set a good example of wanting to do something significant, meaningful, and important with their lives.

Mike seemed to be unconcerned about making lots of friends or being part of a popular crowd, but his easygoing smile drew people to him. I suppose his preppy haircut and athletic physique made him a magnet, especially when he smiled at the ladies with his Kurt Douglas-like dimpled chin. He didn't seem to care about all the female attention he often received—probably because he was already dating one of the most stunning girls in the entire school. He was in the National Honor Society and was a two-sport athlete in high school, playing baseball and football. In order to be friends with Mike, you had to engage him first, but he was more than willing to be friendly once you started the conversation. Since I liked to talk, we got along, and even though we didn't do a whole lot together, I remember going to his home a few times during 1969 and 1970 to spend time with him and his family.

✦

In 1970, right after graduating from high school, Mike and I went on an adventure together to Eastern Oregon and backpacked in the Eagle Cap Wilderness area for about fourteen days. The Eagle Cap Wilderness sits in the heart of the Wallowa mountain range.

Since neither of us owned cars, we had to get to Eastern Oregon any way we could. After some strategic planning, we caught a ride to the Greyhound bus station from Mike's dad and departed Portland at 10:30 p.m. After a dark, bumpy night ride, we arrived in La Grande at 6 in the morning and stashed our packs in the completely deserted bus station before going to a restaurant we called "The Greasy Spoon" for an unhealthy and terrible breakfast. It would take three days for Mike's stomach to recover.

We trotted back to the bus station, fully expecting another bus to be waiting for us, only to be met with a nearly deaf old man driving a Dodge pickup truck. Apparently, this was our mode of transportation to get to Lostine, our jump-off point to the Eagle Cap Wilderness.

We made it to Lostine, where "Charley" dropped us off at the Post Office. We walked to the start of the 17-mile gravel road that stood between us and our wilderness adventure. I commented, "Mike, this town is tiny. There can't be more than a hundred people living here. Also, I have to tell you—that breakfast place you picked back in La Grande was a crappy choice. Next time I get to choose."

"That's fine, John. Looks like we'll have to hitchhike from here to the trailhead. Otherwise, you're guaranteed to have your fancy new hiking boots broken in by the time we get there," Mike replied, as easygoing as ever.

We'd been walking less than a mile when a woman named Georgia providentially drove past and took pity on us. She was the first vehicle to drive by, and we hadn't even solicited a ride. She drove us all the way up the valley for no charge. During the ride, we learned that she had spent the last ten years collecting flowers from the area and pressing them, and was ready to publish a complete guide to the flowers in the Wallowa Mountains. Georgia was truly delightful, and Mike would end up visiting her three or four times when he attended University of Oregon, where she was the director of the Herbarium. After bidding her goodbye with our sincere thanks, Mike and I set out into the wild.

Our first day of hiking on the East Fork of the Lostine River was relatively uneventful. We entered a beautiful valley where the trail crossed a few small mountain streams but eventually took us to Eagle Cap peak. The view farther up the valley was stunning. The meadow grass was green and lush. Meadowlarks serenaded us. Pikas were working hard harvesting the abundant mountain grass they'd need in order to survive the coming winter. Before we even saw them, they would shout as if to say, "I see you."

We set up our base camp at Mirror Lake near the base of the mountain, making a quick dinner and falling asleep at dusk. We were so tuckered out from our travels thus far that we both slept for eleven-and-a-half hours. The next morning we successfully summited Eagle Cap, but encountered a bit of trouble as we crossed the ridge toward Glacier Peak. I decided to hike around a highly exposed ledge with a 2,000-foot drop into the East Fork of Eagle Creek. The wind was blowing and after climbing up a chimney to the top of the ridge, I couldn't hear Mike and he couldn't hear me. While always methodical and careful, he wasn't the strongest climber, so after about twenty nerve-wracking minutes, I was relieved to see him finally appear near the top of the chimney. "Mike, come up this way, I'm at the top of this ridge. Man, I'm so glad you decided to follow me. I was worried that you were going to go back to base camp the way we came and leave me up here to figure out how to get to our camp on my own."

He gave me a frown and said, "John, we need to stick together, and before you go off and do some freehand rock climbing again, let's talk about it first."

As we stood on that rocky ridge, we both realized a large shelf glacier stood between us and a safe route back to camp. I asked Mike, "What's the name of this glacier?"

"I think it's called Benson Glacier." Not wanting to seem worried about our predicament, I said, "I want to summit Glacier Peak before we move our base camp. What do you think?"

"We can do that in the next day or so. Right now we can't go back the way we came, and glissading is not an option. We'd best try to get down off this glacier by making long, back-and-forth switchback turns, and hope like hell we don't slip." Neither of us had crampons. For the next hour or so, not a word was spoken between us. We were totally focused on not slipping and falling. One slip, and it would be a very fast 1,000-foot slide into the rocks below. Miraculously, we made it down to Glacier Pass.

Mike had made the mistake of hiking in the full sun and wind at 9,500 feet of elevation without a shirt on, and as a result he developed what was likely a combination of hypothermia and sunstroke. He went into a bit of shock, ran a fever, and had an upset stomach. After rinsing off in a lake, we returned to our base camp, where we relived our adventurous day while watching the shooting stars and heat lightning. Thankfully, I hadn't encountered any of Mike's maladies, other than a few serious blisters on my feet.

When you sat around a campfire with Mike, you could have a conversation about anything. His opinions were few and far between, but he would participate in the conversation in a way that you felt he was truly interested in whatever you were talking about. Yes, I always talked more than he did, but we got along just fine.

In the morning I was surprised to find Mike remarkably refreshed. "Mike, last night before you called it a night, you looked like crap. I thought for sure you were going to be unable to do much today."

Shooting me a quick smile, he responded, "I actually feel much better; let's go fishing." We hit several lakes, and for the first time in my life I went high mountain lake fishing. Mike was an excellent fisherman and taught me some basic fishing skills, and I was able to catch five brook trout.

Each night for the next eight days we were able to see the stars from horizon to horizon, but a major storm system blew in while we were hiking on the Minam River. That storm brought with it fog, wet snow, and lots of rain. After several hours of what seemed like a nonstop deluge, we both weren't feeling well, so we decided to trek back out of the mountains through the West Lostine River. Frankly, we were nervous that the unfavorable weather would become dangerous, possibly bringing severe thunderstorms or serious amounts of snowfall.

After about a day and a half of hiking, we reached Two Pan, the Forest Service Campground, and encountered several groups of hunters camping there. Two of the hunters were a couple named Larry and Donna. We regaled them with stories of our adventures and, since they were hunting for deer, we told them how many deer we had seen. The weather broke for several hours with overcast skies and heavy mist, and we set up our camp and went to bed feeling safe for the first time in several days.

At 3 a.m., Larry roughly woke us up in the midst of a severe thunderstorm. The adverse weather had returned—lightning and thunder were crackling, and the rain was pouring down so hard it was difficult to see. Larry shouted that the bridges over the Lostine River were going to wash away soon, so if we wanted to get out, he and Donna were willing to give us a ride back to Portland with them. Still disoriented, Mike asked if we could have five minutes to break camp. Larry looked behind him, and then swung back around with a resounding no.

We scrambled to throw on some clothes and tear Mike's tent down, running into the darkness toward the road as quickly as we could. Suddenly, I heard a thump and a groan. Mike had smacked directly into a Douglas fir tree. More cautiously, we groped our way to the road and hopped into Larry and Donna's camper, which was thankfully still there. In all the chaos to catch our ride with Larry and Donna, I left my perfectly broken-in new hiking boots under the picnic table. I still miss those boots.

After a much quicker trip back than it took us to get to the Wallowas, we arrived back in Portland. Larry and Donna even dropped us off on Mike's front steps—true tent-to-door service. I'm not sure what would have happened to us without their intervention.

Our shared adventure was extraordinary, especially hiking in the mountains of the Eagle Cap Wilderness. Mike gave me the opportunity to experience, up close, the majesty of being surrounded by pristine mountains and lakes. With every footstep I took hiking, climbing, bushwhacking, and scrambling up seldom-used trails to reach some mountain summits, I was in awe. We lost touch with one another after our adventure. Yet because we had shared this amazing journey together, one that was unique to just us, our reconnection years later was easy and natural.

At the time of our mountain excursion, the world was in commotion regarding the war in Vietnam. Most newspapers and the evening news programs would report about all the chaos in the world, especially Vietnam. It was almost impossible to be neutral about the war in 1970, especially when you saw on TV that National Guardsmen shot and killed four college students at Kent State University who were among hundreds of students protesting the war. I saw the news, I saw the pictures, but at the time, it all seemed surreal to me. Soon after that incident the singing group Crosby, Stills, Nash, and Young recorded a song written by Neil Young called "Ohio." It became an anthem of sorts for many to stand up and protest the Vietnam War even more.

That year Rob and I were to make our memorable trip in pursuit of the power lines, changing the course of our lives—though we didn't know it yet. Later in the spring of 1971, while attending college in Washington, I received my notice to go take my pre-induction physical for the draft. The government was still drafting young men to fight in the war, and it looked very likely that after I passed the physical I would be heading to Vietnam. I took the bus to Spokane, Washington, and reported to the military facility. I'll never forget how I stood in a long line with many other guys as some doctors examined us. Shortly after, I was told to expect to receive a letter informing me when and where to report to the army. That summer I transferred to another college and waited for the letter requiring me to report for duty. Rob and Mike were both in Oregon.

I was conflicted because Dave was in Vietnam, up on the DMZ (demilitarized zone) trying to survive. I supported his decision to enlist and I wanted him to come home alive and unharmed, yet I really didn't want to follow in his footsteps. However, I knew I might have to, because my draft lottery number was ninety. Soon enough I would have to deal with that problem.

1972 was filled with change. I finished a semester of college in Utah, worked on a cattle ranch that summer in Salmon, Idaho, and returned home to find a job. The letter to report to the army never came. Dave had returned home from Vietnam and finished his military responsibilities in Manhattan, Kansas. Now home, Dave married Rob's sister Deborah.

Around Christmas time, one of the most notable, non-political events of the year (for Rob, Dave, and me, at least) was the release of the movie *Jeremiah Johnson* starring Robert Redford. We were enthralled with the sweeping panoramas of rugged vistas, the unforgettable characters of Jeremiah, Bearclaw Chris Lapp, and Del Gue, and what it meant to live life as a mountain man. There was something unique about the film that resonated with us. Perhaps it was the cinematography or the music, combined with the idea of living in the wilderness far removed from "civilization" that captivated us. Hiking in mountains became our escape from the realities we faced that year.

We went and watched the movie more than once at the theaters. Whether we would admit it or not, we all fancied ourselves as a modern version of the movie character Jeremiah Johnson. Rob was blond like Robert Redford, and Dave was rugged enough to pass for any mountain man he wanted to portray. Rob and I even read the two books the movie was based upon, *Mountain Man* by Vardis Fisher and *Crow Killer: The Saga of Liver-Eating Johnson* by Robert Bunker. The idea of building our own "Jeremiah Johnson" cabin in the wilderness began to formulate.

Then, during the late summer months of 1973, Rob and I trekked back up the trail in the old-growth forest we had become so enamored with and expanded our explorations—hiking on trails, off the trails, and using topographical maps or line-of-sight methods in search for our future cabin site. One day I even volunteered to climb as high as I could up a tall Douglas fir tree to provide a report of what I could see within a mile or two radius. From my vantage point, off in one direction were what looked like some ponds, or perhaps beaver-built lakes, not too far away. We knew there were creeks and streams everywhere. In all directions I could see watersheds[1] to be hiked—there would be water in each one, perhaps even some side streams. A year-round water source was a critical component in our quest for the perfect place. Our search area to build a cabin encompassed many trails and places in the Willamette National Forest. Within that area there are over 1,700 miles of trails leading to hundreds of remote watersheds, which in turn afforded perhaps a few hundred places we could build.

⁂

That March, Dave and Rob decided to explore another trailhead and invited me to join them. It was early spring in the valley, late lingering winter in the mountains. They left for the mountains, but my full-time job working at the local grocery store meant I would go and find them a day later. They promised to leave me a sign on the trail. Their manmade trail barrier would mean I immediately needed to look around for additional signs and make my presence known, because they would be in the woods not far off the trail.

A day before they left, I observed what each had packed for their hike. They were planning to spend two nights, perhaps more.

Rob looked well prepared. His canvas pack had many essentials. He also took with him a nice sized tarp and a typical flannel-lined sleeping bag we commonly used in that era. He had packed a small coffee pot, food, and other essentials.

Dave, on the other hand, seemed to be taking a more stoic approach regarding the contents in his pack—he always was the Spartan of the group. He had clearly decided he wanted to have a pretty light pack. I can't blame him; most trails we had been exploring contained long steep stretches and lots of elevation gain. He wasn't even taking a traditional sleeping bag with him. Instead he was going to bring his 1970s version of the space blanket.[4]

When they took off on their hike, the weather was rainy, cold, and windy. When I got to the trail the next day, the weather wasn't much better. I was prepared for bad weather. My pack was extraordinarily heavy and bulky. I actually brought along an extra sleeping bag for Dave. I also brought some incredible steaks from the meat market next to the grocery store where I worked and a loaf of Carl Dixon's butter crust unsliced bread.

I had never hiked this trail previously, so I didn't know what to expect. I got a late start and arrived at the trailhead knowing I was going to run out of daylight sooner than I would have preferred. There was no one on the trail. Not a soul. The rain had picked up in intensity. I had things carefully packed both inside and outside my canvas hiking pack, so the things that needed to stay dry were going to be dry. I was determined we would have a feast for dinner that night.

What began as a gradual climb up this unknown trail quickly became steep and arduous. I grew tired but kept my head down and made progress. I found myself resting quite often due to the heavy weight on my back, but I was hoping to get to the spot where they would have barricaded the trail before dark. The climb kept getting steeper, with not enough switchbacks and too many long grades.

The rain wouldn't let up. In the dense forest, darkness comes early. Starting to lose sight of the trail, I broke out my flashlight. Finally, I reached a spot where the trail started leveling off. I had been climbing for over four hours. In my mind I'd hiked at least four, maybe six miles.

I was growing very weary of this adventure. All I wanted was to find my friends. I knew Rob's tarp was large and I was certain it would provide adequate shelter from any downpour. Speaking of downpours—this one didn't seem to want to let up. I wasn't sure if they'd have a campfire in this wretched rainstorm, but I hoped they would.

Plodding forward a few hundred yards, I finally came upon several logs propped up in such a way that they seemed to be an unmistakable man-made barrier informing me this was the spot where I needed to look around in hopes of finding Rob and Dave. Immediately, I shouted as loud as I could. Listening for a moment, I soon heard shouts coming back to me in the distance. I shouted again and to my surprise their shouts were coming toward me. I was now off the trail, stumbling and tripping as I rushed forward to the sound of their voices.

The hike had been physically and psychologically demanding. I felt a huge sense of relief when Dave greeted me. Almost immediately he took my pack and expressed how glad he was that I made it. His emotions were a surprise to me at the time; Dave rarely expressed his feelings in an excited manner. I soon found out why he was so excited.

Walking a few hundred more yards, I finally arrived at their primitive shelter. Indeed, it was a "lean-to." At the high end of the structure one could stand up. On the low end, the lean-to poles rested upon a large, wind fallen tree about two feet in diameter.

The fire they had built looked odd. Clearly, dry wood was scarce. Using some ingenuity they had started a small fire and quickly shielded it from the rainstorm by stacking split pieces of wood in a crisscross fashion. The actual fire itself was rather small and didn't put out much heat. The pile of stacked wood to protect the fire was at least four feet high, while the fire itself only generated flames about a foot or so off the ground. Depending on which way the wind was blowing, you either had a face full of smoke—

which forced you to move away from the shelter into the rain—or you would sit under the shelter hoping the fire would finally generate enough heat to make you feel actually warm, instead of chilled and near the point of shivering.

I began unpacking and exposing all the gear I had brought. A huge grin came across Dave's face as he saw that I'd packed more than one sleeping bag, in addition to steaks, bread, canned food, and additional cooking utensils. "John, you are good man to carry so much stuff up the trail." That night, after the campfire was stoked properly, we had a feast: New York steaks cooked to perfection, freeze-dried mashed potatoes, Carl Dixon's butter crust unsliced bread, and some Lady Alberta peaches.

As we stood around the campfire with full bellies, our conversation went multiple directions. Both Rob and Dave continued to stoke the fire with many more logs stacked several feet high. We all wanted to have the fire going in the morning. I was confident that the fire builders would be the fire keepers this night.

The sounds of the evening were not quiet in the least. The rain was subsiding a bit, but the wind continued to blow hard out of the west, and because this forest was so dense and the trees stood so close together, they made their own kind of music as their branches banged against each other. There is something soothing about the sound the wind makes as it blows through the treetops, serenading anyone there to listen.

I made sure both Rob and Dave knew how much I had their backs by bringing up so much food and gear, and both of them made sure I knew how grateful they were. I asked, "Hey Rob, how did Dave do with his space blanket?"

"Well as the night wore on, I was worried he was going to expect me to share my sleeping bag with him."

Acting offended, Dave interjected, "How would you know? You were sound asleep. It was your snoring that kept me awake—I was just fine."

Rob laughed. "Right, is that why I felt you snuggling up against me late last night? Or was that a black bear that happened to wander into our lean-to?" Considering the banter I was hearing back and forth between those two, it seemed that the night before had been a tough go for Dave with his space blanket experiment. As the campfire threw off a considerable amount of light through the darkness, I caught a look on Rob's face that told me I had come to their rescue, or at least Dave's.

Morning did bring with it a skiff of snow on the ground. True to form, the campfire had been burning the entire night. A fresh water source was found about fifty yards away; water for coffee had already been fetched and breakfast-making activities had begun by the time I hauled my tired bones out of my sleeping bag. The weather had improved quite a bit since the day before. As I looked around my surroundings, I observed the lean-to-shelter in its entirety. As is most often the case, Rob has a knack for building things and making things comfortable, especially out in the woods. With Dave's help, their shelter would do. We would use the lean-to off and on for the next six years.

After breakfast we went exploring farther on the main trail, up to the highest point we could reach. This trail, like most of the other trails we had hiked, seemed to climb considerably in elevation, going miles deeper into the Willamette National Forest and providing us ample opportunities to get away from the chaos of the so-called civilized world and the mundane reality of the small-town life we lived in 1973.

A

To find a proper place for a proper cabin, in the summer of 1974 Rob and I went hiking together and decided to start bushwhacking. Bushwhacking is not really hiking. First, there is no trail, and for some compelling reason you've decided to leave a maintained trail to explore a part of the forest which is filled with bushes and downed trees. You're definitely not walking; you're climbing over and under fallen trees. Sometimes you're swimming through vine maple. You may have no choice but to wade or ford across a creek. The whole point of bushwhacking is to explore, to almost get lost. You may or may not be heading toward anything in particular. Then again, your bushwhacking efforts may result in finding the perfect place to build a cabin.

While bushwhacking, we saw a little game trail and followed it as it sloped gradually downhill for about a half mile, maybe less. The land continued to drop abruptly for thirty to fifty feet to an area with a small grove of cedar trees. On one edge of that tiny cedar grove was a big cedar tree. It was colossal, making a great reference point. It had a diameter of at least fifteen feet and towered above the rest of the trees. It could have been 200 feet tall. After stopping to admire its sheer majesty, we took our next compass heading to where we thought a lake would be on our topographical map and followed that point—bushwhacking again—off to our right, where we saw a boggy area full of vine maple, devil's club, and other stuff to avoid. On our left, we followed the terrain as it gradually sloped upward again. We realized a spring flowed year-round in the wet, boggy area, becoming a creek. We crossed that little creek and kept on our compass heading. We fought our way through a barrier of bushes that acts as natural habitat to guard many mountain lakes, and discovered our theoretical lake was, in fact, real. We saw how pristine it was, and realized as we tried to walk around its edge that we could see where large trees had been gnawed and knocked down by beavers. After a closer examination, we concluded that beavers built this lake.

On the other side of the lake was a meadow. I wouldn't call it a pasture by any means, but a meadow that stayed pretty wet year-round. Maybe in late August it would be dry enough to walk across without getting our feet wet. We roamed around the area rejoicing in the fact that we had found the lake, and realized we had discovered a special spot that we could possibly consider as the place to build our long-awaited cabin.

People are often motivated to justify their actions, beliefs, and feelings to eliminate a conflict they may have. This was true re-garding the idea of building a cabin on public land, and when the decision was eventually made to build the cabin back in the early 1970s, the government had allowed for structures to be built and maintained in the National Forest, provided certain criteria were met. In the case of the cabin, the intent was to obtain a permit. That option vanished when the National Forest re-designated the desired location to a "special management area." The justification for building a cabin (back then) became grounded in the belief that the actual cabin itself would be available for use by anyone who knew its whereabouts or found it, thereby becoming public proper-ty. The conflict was resolved.

Rob and I returned back to the trail a similar way we'd come, once again encountered the Big Cedar Tree, and concluded it was an important landmark in order for people to find this place again. Little did we know the number of times we would pass by this sen-tinel during the next fifty years.

Chapter 4
Friendships Made.
Friendships Rekindled.

"Many people will walk in and out of your life, but only true friends will leave footprints in your heart." —Eleanor Roosevelt

After Rob and I returned from our trek, our mountain explorations would be put on hold for a couple of years.

Dave's marriage to Rob's younger sister Deborah further strengthened his and Rob's bond. Dave was very busy finishing his college degree, getting his teaching credentials, and helping to raise his young family. He went on to teach health and fitness at a junior high school in the Willamette Valley, as well as coach the cross country and girl's basketball teams. As it was with everything Dave did, he excelled in both coaching and teaching. From 1975 to 1977 Rob was away going to college, and I was off living in Louisiana and Mississippi serving a mission for my church.

As expected, Rob excelled in his academic and athletic pursuits while at college. He ran collegiate cross-country and track. He even considered going to medical school, but later told me he didn't think a career in medicine was a good fit for him and instead pursued graduate studies in bioengineering. After earning his master's degree, he accepted a full-time engineering position in California.

⚘

Meanwhile, athough I wasn't communicating with Mike regularly, I knew he had worked in his father's family business during high school summers and every summer during college. He also worked at an Italian restaurant for several years. He truly worked his way through college, paying for his own education. He went to University of Oregon and graduated with a degree in some sort of business management.

⚜

In June of 1975, I met Terry while we were full-time missionaries laboring in the New Orleans area. Originally from North Dakota, Terry was a passionate and devoted missionary who gave service to many people in Louisiana and Mississippi. When we served together he was very kind and respectful to everyone. He was full of zeal and passion about sharing his faith in Jesus Christ, but he never forced his faith on anyone. Bright-eyed and energetic, he willingly looked for ways to serve others and made a positive difference in the lives of many people, including mine. For someone who was nineteen when I first met him, he acted more like somebody who was twenty-nine years old. We were constantly together and shared some amazing experiences.

I've never forgotten Halloween night in 1975. Terry and I were roommates in Metairie, Louisiana, a suburb of New Orleans, staying in an apartment that was rented by the Emergency Room Chief Resident at Charity Hospital in New Orleans. He was leaving town to do a medical rotation at another hospital, so he needed someone to stay in his apartment for a few months. His place was much nicer than where Terry and I were originally staying, so we jumped at the chance to apartment-sit his nice accommodations. A few months later, he invited us to visit the hospital and see firsthand what it was like to be an emergency room doctor. We finally took him up on his offer and went on Halloween night.

The New Orleans Charity Hospital (in those days) treated an average of twenty-five stabbing or gunshot wound victims per night. It was the busiest or second busiest Charity Hospital in the country. It's called a Charity Hospital because they don't turn people away. Therefore, they get the people who don't have insurance, are off the street, drug addicts, prostitutes, and people who don't have any other options for medical care.

Terry was nineteen, and I had turned twenty-four in July. We walked into the hospital through the emergency room entrance and a guy at the front desk was very accommodating; he paged the ER Chief Resident, who came to where we were and asked us to follow him around for the night. We said yes, and he instructed us to get on some hospital scrubs and prepare to help if needed.

Our evening started with cutting sutures for him while he was stitching people up. Of course we weren't licensed to do any of those sorts of things, and I found it completely unexpected. Terry jumped right into it; as always, he was passionate about helping and engaging everyone who was receiving care. "Terry, you seemed so relaxed. I had to avert my eyes and tune out the pained sounds that young woman was making."

"Listen John, if we can help the doctor attend to more people tonight, then that's a good thing. Keep focused on that truth, then you'll do just fine."

As we conversed about the circumstances in which we found ourselves, a young man who had fired off his 12-gauge shotgun while getting out of his car arrived by ambulance. He had accidentally pulled the trigger and blown most of his leg off. We could see the bone because the muscle was gone, but his foot was still attached with a boot on it. The paramedics had him stabilized, so we just wheeled him back to the OR. Later, some surgeon amputated his leg. Next, a woman came into the ER. She probably had a very beautiful face, but she had run into trouble with someone who cut her face up with a straight-edge razor, and parts of her face looked like Swiss cheese. Her cheeks were slashed open exposing her flesh—it was a horrible, tragic situation. She was screaming in pain and we were instructed to press some sterile gauze in places where she was bleeding until she could be taken into surgery. Thankfully, an orderly came and transported her to get stitched up by the plastic surgeon on call.

Another young woman came in who could hardly breathe. Apparently she had developed such a severe case of tonsillitis that she was gasping for breath. The attending doctor was afraid she was going to stop breathing. The medical team thought it might be anaphylaxis but it wasn't—the infection was just that extreme. A trauma surgeon showed up and reached in with his scalpel, no anesthesia or anything. With very little hesitation, he cut her tonsils out to give her an airway. She screamed, but he probably saved her life. After that they rushed her back to the OR to put her back together. The trauma cases seemed to never stop.

When we went back to the waiting room, another woman had just been escorted in by police from a bar fight. She had pulled a gun on somebody and fired but missed, and one of the bullets ricocheted off the floor right into her own rear end. She was not a small woman by any means, weighing probably 300 pounds or more, so they weren't sure where the bullet was lodged or what type of damage had been done.

Terry and I were standing there, these naive missionaries in a medical procedure room, with this woman laying on the examination table stark naked. They finally draped the woman while the attending surgical resident tried to thread a needle into her femoral artery in order to be able to run an arteriogram and assess the situation, but she had such big thighs he had trouble finding the artery and made three attempts to locate it. They didn't have an ultrasound machine. When he inserted the needle and finally found the artery, blood shot all over. Some went on the wall, some hit him directly in the face, and for a couple seconds it was just squirting everywhere. I thought to myself, "Welcome to Charity Hospital."

In six hours' time Terry and I had definitely shared an unexpected and eye-opening experience—something so different from our usual missionary activities that it created an unbreakable bond of friendship between us.

After Terry's mission, he became a paramedic. He was planning to attend medical school but for some reason changed his mind and applied to dental school instead. He even completed a hospital-based residency as a dental resident. We could have gone our whole lives without seeing some of the medical trauma we saw that night at Charity Hospital; it was literally a haunting Halloween for me.

During my time as a missionary in Louisiana and parts of Mississippi, I came to realize that I had lived a sheltered life in our small town in Oregon. My high school graduating class only contained three African Americans. In the New Orleans area, the population was about 60 percent African American. When we rode buses for public transportation, we sat right alongside our African-American brothers and sisters. Once, as we were boarding a city bus, the driver said to us, "Back of the bus, Whitey." That didn't bother me. If anything, it made me realize that forms of racism and discrimination still existed, but because of the civil rights movement of the 1960s, important social changes were happening for the better. At least, I hoped they were.

After our missionary service, I returned home to Oregon and Terry returned home to North Dakota where he grew up. I was quickly able to find some work as an unskilled laborer in Portland, Oregon. It didn't take long before I realized I needed to find a better job and look for employment opportunities elsewhere. While traveling with some friends to Utah, I was introduced to a girl named Lauren. We began a whirlwind romance and after a short courtship got married in July of 1977. We moved to Central California, where she was from, and I took a job working in their HVAC heating and air conditioning business.

✦

Sometime in late 1977 or the early part of 1978, I became friends with Lloyd (Mac, as almost everyone called him). He was a commercial airline pilot and when he wasn't flying for work he was busy with family life, playing golf or tennis, and other recreational activities.

I would turn twenty-seven in July 1978, and had been trying to get back to a high level of fitness. Back in high school and before my mission, physical fitness had been a part of my DNA (Daily Normal Activities), or at least I thought so. I regularly ran three to six miles four days a week. When I wasn't working, I played a lot of tennis and hiked in the mountains regularly. While living in Oregon, Rob, Dave, and I regularly went water skiing in the spring, summer, and fall months of the year. Regrettably, I had gained over twenty pounds while living in Louisiana, and I wanted to lose that weight.

Mac was a very active man. Although he was nineteen years my senior, we hit it off and became friends. One day we played some tennis and I told him about a half marathon race held in Spray, Oregon. After discovering he had never been to Central Oregon, I raved about the scenic beauty and asked if he'd be interested in running the half marathon with me. Dave and Rob, whom I hadn't seen in over a year, were also planning on participating. Mac said yes, and even suggested that we fly in his single-engine plane to get there. The next thing I knew, we were running together early in the mornings three times a week. Three months flew by, and just after sunrise the morning of May 26th, we left Modesto, California, en route to John Day, Oregon, in his Mooney airplane. The airport in John Day was so small that they didn't have any rental cars; instead, they had two loaner cars to choose from. The better of the two was a four-door 1965 Buick. We could borrow it as long as we brought it back with more gas in the tank than when we started.

The eighty-mile drive to the start of the half marathon was incredibly scenic. The John Day River provides water for cattle ranchers to grow and harvest hay, alfalfa, and other crops. The first deep-green, lush cutting of alfalfa was already being harvested that year. For nearly 300 miles, this undammed river meanders from the Strawberry Mountains to the Columbia River. As it makes its way to the Columbia, it passes through sleepy little towns like John Day, Mt. Vernon, Dayville, Kimberly, and Spray. Each is unique with a story to tell. The road to Spray follows the river, and each town carves out most of its existence from the resources the river provides. We passed by the John Day Fossil Beds and stopped at the Painted Hills to take in their rare geological beauty with yellows, golds, blacks, and reds. The hills are stunningly beautiful and the yellow wildflowers of spring added more color as they bloomed in open areas of the hills themselves.

The race itself took place on a fun course, on Hwy 19 as it meanders along the Middle Fork of the John Day River from Service Creek to Spray. The day after we arrived, just before the start of the race, we met up with Rob and Dave, and I introduced them to Mac. I was bursting with excitement and had lost nearly twelve pounds during my training for this race. As was always the case, Rob and Dave fit in the elite category and could easily average 6-plus minute miles over the 13-mile distance. I was hoping to average a pace of eight to nine minutes per mile. When the starting gun went off and the crowd of about 150 runners took off, I was so amped up that I actually kept pace with Dave and Rob. . .for the first mile. Soon, I realized running with the big boys was a big mistake; I quickly slowed way down to the pace I had trained my body to run. Mac caught up with me at about the 9-mile mark. He would finish before I did.

As I approached the finish line, I heard Mac, Rob, and Dave cheering. "Way to finish, John," Rob called. Lumbering across the finish line, I took a moment to catch my breath.

Seeing Mac, I said, "Mac, you're amazing. When you passed me you looked like you were in a running trance. Did you hear me say, 'Reel some more people in, Mac'?"

"Sorry John, I don't remember that. I did meet up with your buddies Rob and Dave at the finish line, though." We headed over to the elementary school for a mid-day pancake breakfast sponsored by the town locals. Afterwards we all walked down to the river and rinsed off our sweat and grime. It was good to see Rob and Dave again. We all seemed to be pleased with our race results, and agreed that we'd run this race again sometime.

🔱

Sadly, my marriage to Lori lasted only a few years, but we did have two beautiful children. It was an emotionally difficult time for me. My marriage failed, and I share part of the responsibility for that. I continued to live in Central California to be close to my kids. I didn't particularly enjoy working in residential real estate, so I went to work for a property-casualty independent insurance agency. Central California was not the Pacific Northwest, nor was it home to me. I knew that eventually I would return to my beloved Willamette Valley of Oregon.

Chapter 5
Perfect Place Found

"Unlike Muir and Thoreau, McCandless went into the wilderness not primarily to ponder nature or the world at large but, rather, to explore the inner country of his own soul."
—Jon Krakauer (Into the Wild)

In the spring of 1979, Rob and Dave started re-exploring different parts of the Willamette National Forest. They went on several scouting trips searching for a new location—the perfect location for a real cabin (one with a floor) to replace the old lean-to, which had been in use since our trip in the spring of 1973. The old lean-to was damp, drippy, smoky, and cold, without adequate headroom. It had also been ransacked a couple of times by bears, which was not surprising since it was not enclosed.

On this particular trip, Dave and Rob decided to go back to the area near the lean-to and explore further to determine if there was a spot far enough from any maintained trails, somewhere that a proper wilderness cabin—a Jeremiah Johnson-style cabin—could be built. It would have a stove to supply heat, and while storms might rage outside, it would be dry inside with a wood floor so that we could walk around toasty warm in our stocking feet.

They did a lot of bushwhacking and finally found the Big Cedar Tree that served as an essential landmark toward the beaver-built lake Rob and I had located years before. But on this particular trip there was one problem: Where could Rob and Dave easily cross the creek, which at the time was swollen with spring runoff? The entire area was about 50 percent covered with snow and ice. Even though the snow was melting quickly because of the continuous spring rains, the stream was easily a foot or more deep and seven to ten feet wide in places. Their "only problem" was solved when Rob found a natural bridge over the creek just a hundred yards above the lake. That natural bridge was formed from the top part of a big

cedar snag, which may have been killed in the wildfires that rav-
aged the area in about 1920. The bridge part of the tree was about
four feet in diameter where it laid across the creek, and the stump
end of the snag was about eight feet in diameter at its buttressed
base. The huge old stump was quite striking, so much so that Rob
and Dave decided to situate the cabin with its front door facing the
beautiful natural cedar bridge.

Rob and Dave decided that Providence had reserved this place
especially for the building of the cabin, and real plans began to
form. When they looked around at the cabin site and used their
imaginations, it was not too difficult to feel in some small measure the way the pioneers must have felt when they opened up a
trackless wilderness. Except, this wasn't the 1870s. It was over a
hundred years later, and both the State and Federal government
had new rules about building on public land. It didn't matter that
the Willamette National Forest was so vast and covered over a 1.5
million acres of land. What harm would a small cabin situated on
less than an acre really cause? At this time in America, many of our
generation had become a part of a social revolt against government
intrusion into our lives. Rob's dilemma was that he wanted to build
a cabin in the forest, but the government said it was now against the
law to do so. The decision of civil disobedience began as a benign
action, with a commitment to only use nature's discarded excess resources to build a small shelter, a tiny cabin. H. D. Thoreau would
have been proud. Rob and Dave were not hippies, just modern-day
Jeremiah-Johnson-wannabes.

When they camped on the future site of the cabin, Rob and
Dave cleared some downed timber and built their first campfire
near the creek. Knowing that the perfect place to build had finally
been found, they started work on the foundation and made the decision to return in a week to continue construction, with the hope
that the drenching rain would let up by then.

Tools and supplies needed to be brought to the cabin site. Small
tools like a froe[5] or a couple of axes could be easily carried in a
backpack. Preparing for his return to continue cabin construction,

Rob filled his pack with tools and food. The pack weighed between fifty to seventy-five pounds. It was essential to have a two-man crosscut saw up at the cabin site. Rob knew that and was not shy about the fact that he would have to carry it in a very unusual manner up the trail. Rob secured the pack on his back and carefully took the misery whip,[6] then bent it into the shape of a horseshoe. The bowed crosscut saw was mostly above his head and shoulders, and after taking one handle in each of his hands, he began making his journey.

The trail for the first mile is well traveled and the path is actually three to four feet wide, free of obstacles, which enabled him to hike that section without much difficulty. The next three miles would be challenging. Rob would have to walk sideways up the trail in places, and in others he would need to reposition the saw in order to traverse over some rocks or mudslides that blocked the trail from being navigated in a normal manner. If you were hiking the trail that day and encountered him with his saw bent above his head, you would have had a sight to behold.

Resuming construction, Rob and Dave placed the cornerstones and cedar sill logs. The cabin was entirely built without the use of power tools. This initial decision was made with the intent to replicate what pioneers actually had experienced, and also to reflect a mutual respect for the environment.

Building a log cabin from surrounding trees in a dense forest is a small logging operation. Logging can be messy and unsightly. The nearby stream (which flowed a few feet away) sacrificed several rocks for the placement of the foundation and the sill logs to rest upon. Using the misery whip and the axes, they cut and stacked enough logs that first day to finish the walls up to the cap-over. That top log would eventually support the log rafters and the roof. All the logs were cut from standing dead trees. They put floor joists in place and finished the roof purlins (the top of the cabin walls). Soon, the rafters would be secured to those walls and the making of cedar shingles would commence. Dave was only able to stay for a few days helping Rob because he had to get back to town and attend to his family responsibilities. I was living in California during that time and was not able to help build the original cabin.

Rob would finish the walls by himself, and for several months he continued making treks to the cabin. He was resolute and determined to finish his Jeremiah Johnson cabin before winter set in. He spent a majority of the summer and fall months there all alone, sometimes staying a week or more at a time in order to make his cabin dream become a reality.

Next on the building agenda was to construct and shingle the roof. Fortunately, about a hundred yards away from the cabin were several old cedar trees that had blown over from some windstorm. These cedar logs were perfect for making shingles and other cabin necessities. However, the bigger task was to harvest all the cedar bolts, which are small lengths of western red cedar which can be later processed into cedar shingles or shakes. Each bolt was about five to six feet long and twenty-four to thirty-six inches in diameter. It usually took two people to transport each bolt back to the cabin. That journey would entail some serious effort to navigate all the forest obstacles that existed between the harvesting site and the cabin. Some of the bolts of lumber weighed over 200 pounds. Eventually, a peavey was brought up to the cabin. A peavey usually is a pointed stick with a movable side claw to grasp and maneuver logs of varying diameters. This tool made harvesting cedar bolts much less physically demanding. Depending upon your point of view, making the bolts of cedar into shakes was easy work compared to harvesting the cedar bolts and getting them back to the cabin.

Of course, Rob could have harvested some live cedar trees that were near the cabin, making it really easy from a physical work aspect. Yet that was against the code of conduct—the way we all viewed our responsibility to the forest and the environment. Near the cabin, a large fallen log was modified for "bucking logs" and became the cabin sawbuck. A sawbuck is a special kind of sawhorse framed for holding rough logs so they can be sawed into lengths suitable for use in a stove, fireplace, or the walls or beams of a cabin.

Rob's brother Brad came to be a part of the original cabin-building experience and became a cedar shake-making machine. The cabin would finally get roofed, and despite my best efforts, I could never describe the splitting of cedar shingles as beautifully as Daniel James Brown does in his book *The Boys in the Boat*.

Charlie led Joe among the stumps and downed trees, teaching him how to understand what lay beneath the bark of the fallen logs. He rolled them over with a peavey and pounded them with the flat face of a splitting maul, testing for the ringing tone that indicated soundness. He ran his hands over them, feeling for hidden knots and irregularities. He crouched down at the cut ends and peered at the annual growth rings, trying to get a nuanced read on how tight and regular the grain within was likely to be. Joe was fascinated, intrigued by the idea that he could learn to see what others could not see in the wood, thrilled as always at the notion that something valuable could be found in what others had passed over and left behind. When Charlie found a log he liked, and explained to Joe why he liked it, the two of them used a crosscut saw to buck the wood into twenty-four inch bolts—sections the length of a roofing shake—and toted them back to the buckboard.

Later Charlie taught Joe how to decipher the subtle clues of shape, texture, and color that would enable him to cleave the wood into well-formed shakes, to see hidden points of weakness or resilience. He taught the younger man how to split a log neatly into quarters with a maul and iron wedges; how to use a heavy wooden mallet to pound a froe—the shake maker's principal tool: a long, straight blade with an equally long perpendicular handle—into the wood across rather than with the grain; how to work the froe evenly down the length of the wood; how to listen to the wood as it began to "talk" back to him, the fibers crackling and snapping softly as they pulled away from one another, telling him that they were prepared to split along the plane he intended; how to twist the froe into the wood decisively at just the right moment to make the shake pop free, clean and elegant, smooth faced and gently tapered from one end to the other, ready to put on a roof.

Within a few days, Joe had mastered the froe and the mallet and could size up a log and split shakes from it nearly as quickly and decisively as Charlie could. A year of rowing had given him prodigious strength in his arms and shoulders, and he worked his way through a pile of cedar bolts like a machine. A small mountain of shakes soon surrounded him in the McDonalds' barnyard. Proud of his new skill, he found that shaping cedar resonated with him in an elusive but elemental way—it satisfied him down in his core, and gave him peace. Partly it was the old pleasure that he always derived mastering new tools and solving practical problems—working out the angles and planes at which the cedar would or wouldn't cleave cleanly. And partly it was the deeply sensuous nature of the work. He liked the way that the wood murmured to him before it parted, almost as if it was alive, and when it finally gave way under his hands he liked the way it invariably revealed itself in lovely and unpredictable patterns of color—streaks of orange and burgundy and cream. At the same moment, as the wood opened up, it always perfumed the air. The spicy-sweet aroma that rose from freshly split cedar was the same scent that often filled the shell house in Seattle when Pocock was at work up in his loft. There seemed to Joe to be some kind of connection between what

Stack of Cedar Shakes

he was doing here among a pile of freshly split shakes, what Pocock was doing in his shop, and what he was trying to do himself in the racing shells Pocock built—something about the deliberate application of strength, the careful coordination of mind and muscle, the sudden unfolding of mystery and beauty.

Having made enough shingles for the roof, Rob and Brad finished the eaves and cleaned up the entrance. They were ready to begin roofing, but Rob had forgotten the roofing nails! Rob headed down the trail that night to obtain the galvanized nails necessary to secure the fancy new handmade cedar shingles to the roof. When he returned the next morning, he and Brad shingled the roof. It looked great with long, thin shakes. Soon thereafter Rob installed a nice tin woodstove (shepherd's stove) with the kitchen counter and shelves, all made of cedar.

The original cabin door was built out of heavy cedar boards, with cross members top and bottom, which were securely nailed in place to add strength. The door had two layers of boards more than two inches thick, so the door was actually over four inches thick at the top and bottom. Special efforts were also made to make the door smooth on the outside, and the door even opened outward so as to prevent bears from getting a purchase on the wood or forcing the door in. Rob and Dave spent a lot of time, effort, and labor to make the cabin secure, with the front door as well as a heavy shutter over the window.

🔺

During the initial building of the cabin, a temporary fire pit was built to burn slash (tree limbs and bark) from the logging operation and for cooking. It would be there for several years until Rob built a fancy, oyster-amphitheater-shaped outdoor fireplace.

Rob has many abilities and had developed a special talent for building rock walls, outdoor fireplaces, and hearths made of rocks, all without any mortar. In the beautiful Lake District of England, they have rock wall fences to separate property boundaries. Most are centuries old, rugged and built to last. Rob had been to England and Ireland in the years since high school; perhaps his inspiration and passion for building with rocks came from there?

When he built and then later rebuilt the beautiful outdoor fireplace, any appreciative observer could see that many hours had gone into finding all the rocks needed and placing each rock in just the proper spot. This required patience to make the fireplace functional and yet visually appealing, one of Rob's goals.

🔥

The cabin would usher in the 1980 New Year alone. Rob left for Canada, Washington D.C., and then Ireland, and did not return to Oregon until Christmas of 1980. Dave was in Oregon, Terry was in North Dakota, and I was still living Central California.

🔥

"On May 18th, 1980, an earthquake struck below the north face of Mount St. Helens in nearby Washington State, triggering perhaps the largest landslide in recorded history and a major volcanic eruption that scattered ash across a dozen states. The blast was heard hundreds of miles away and it removed 1,300 feet off the top of the mountain, sending shockwaves and ash, rocks, and lava flows across the surrounding landscape, flattening forests, melting snow and ice, and generating massive mudflows."[7] The Mount St. Helens volcano "didn't just erupt out of its vent at the summit; a huge internal pressure build up and had nowhere to go but sideways, and the volcano obliterated itself by forcing its contents out of its side in a devastating lateral blast."[8]

When I saw news of the Mount St. Helens eruption, with its vivid videos and pictures, I was shaken and concerned for my family and friends. Later I was greatly relieved to learn that everyone who lived in the greater Portland, Oregon, area, eighty miles away to the southwest, was not in the direct path of the blast zone.

Dave may have been up to the cabin several times that year, but no journal record or other source exists to confirm that he was there. Perhaps he decided to just stay the hell out of the mountains, especially considering that Mount St. Helens would erupt again on May 25th, June 12th, and July 22nd, each time sending considerable amounts of ash, rocks, and other particles into the sky—sometimes ten miles above the top of the mountain. I know I would have stayed away.

Chapter 6
The Trail

*"Do not follow where the path may lead. Go instead
where there is no path and leave a trail."*
—*Ralph Waldo Emerson*

Rob, Mike, Dave, Terry, and I have made the physically difficult trek to the cabin many times (some more than others) to
improve and preserve it, and in our own way immerse ourselves
in nature and contend with the elements from time to time. I loved
taking that challenge; it had a transformative effect upon me. I've
never had those same feelings or emotions when hiking elsewhere,
and I've hiked in many other remote wilderness places.

As we liked various lines from *Jeremiah Johnson*, we adopted
some of the dialogue in our communication because we found it a
perfect way to express our feelings under certain circumstances.
For example, whenever any of us approached the cabin site and
knew one of us would be there already, we would shout out the
phrase, "What's on the spit?" The person at the cabin, hearing that
greeting, would respond back, "Grown particular?" Then the reply
back would be, "not about feedin', just the company I keep."

In 2010, I asked Rob if he could give an accurate count of
how many times he had hiked the trail over the past forty years.
He claimed after forty-plus years of hiking the trail to the cabin,
he held the record for making the journey. If his unsubstantiated
record is true (400 trips), then he will have walked, jogged, ran, or
strolled over [4.5x2x400] 3,600 miles in the rain, snow, sunshine,
and other weather elements. This would be like Rob having hiked
from Anchorage, Alaska, to Halifax, Nova Scotia. I have personally made the trek to the cabin about 120 times and that would be
as if I had hiked from Vancouver, British Columbia, to Los Angles,
California, which is a distance of 1,080 miles.

✦

"March is a muddy month down below. Some folks like it, farmers mostly."[1]

The trail leading to the cabin is a beast. There are several hiking groups that like to use the trail for fitness training and preparation for mountain climbing. They seem to like the fact that the trail itself climbs nearly 4,000 feet in elevation over the span of just over four and a half miles.

The first half mile of the hike is rather tame, with a gradual elevation change. This part of the trail is easily maintained and the path itself is seldom overgrown, but then the mountainside becomes very steep. Whoever originally blazed and built the trail must have believed big game animals knew how to climb up the hillside better than humans, and decided to follow some mountain goat path or a game trail created by deer or elk. The steepness of the terrain demanded that several switchback segments be built. Each of those segments was defined by the mountainside's topography. The trail passes under various rocky outcroppings, with some places so narrow from erosion they leave you to wonder how much longer they will last before needing to be rerouted.

In the span of almost fifty years, the trail has taken a beating. Nature has its way of redefining the landscape. There have been many years when we had to traverse over or around rockslides from heavy spring rains and navigate under, around, or over fallen trees from windstorms. I personally like the fact that the trail itself changed from year to year—a little bit here, a little bit there.

Whenever I journeyed up the trail I always looked around to see what had changed since the last time. There is something special about each season of the year on the trail. Throughout the spring you expect rain more often than not. The Willamette Valley is in full, flowery bloom, with the rhododendrons and azalea blossoms presenting a kaleidoscope of colors. Every native flower imaginable bursts forth, expressing their beauty before your eyes. Almost everywhere you look, most colors of the rainbow are on display with all the various flowers in bloom. The usual ground-cover of ferns and other bushes are green and lush along the trail.

Many times I have needed to brush several spider webs back from my face while hiking the trail; it brings a measure of elation to know that no other humans are on the trail ahead of me. Early on in our relationship, I made friends with the trail to the cabin. I proved that I belonged there and wasn't merely passing through because some wilderness or hiking critic said, "Here are the top ten nature hikes in the Pacific Northwest."

On many trails, several stopping or resting spots exist en route to one's destination. The same is true for the hike to the cabin. There are four major stopping or resting spots along the trail. Each is unique, providing a different perspective while hiking up the trail. The first has a lovely view of the forest below and the river in the distance. Here we always offloaded our packs for a brief rest and went searching for the correct outside pocket, which con-tained either an apple or an orange, and possibly some cookies, too. Homemade were always the preferred choice, especially those made by my wife Sandy.

Sandy and I had come to know each other through my friendship with Mac. She was his oldest daughter, and when he and I first became friends, I may have been introduced to Sandy and her four siblings, but can't really even remember when that happened. Back then, my relationship with Mac almost entirely centered around playing tennis, racquetball, or occasionally golf together.

Almost six years had passed since Mac had become my friend, when I came to take notice of Sandy. My realization was like I'd been struck by lightning; there she was, this beautiful and vibrant young woman who lit up a room with her positive energy. People were drawn to her and liked to be in her company. I sure did. As I came to know her better, it became evident to me that she possessed an amazing faith and a deep devotion to her family, which I found incredibly attractive. She was authentic, genuine, and mature beyond her years.

Having been married previously, and as a divorced father of two young children, I was working hard to feel good about remarrying again. I wanted to have something of value to offer and feel worthy enough for someone to love me. I wasn't sure if Sandy would even be interested in me. Nevertheless, I took a leap of faith and looked for ways to be around her. I went to her place of employment (a 1980s version of Office Depot) or her parents' house hoping she would be there, just to have a reason to see and talk to her. I would even call her on the phone (pre-cell phone era) asking if she could look up someone's phone number for me from our congregation's membership directory, which I had, of course, conveniently left at home.

After a couple of months, I finally mustered up enough courage to ask her on a date and we continued to date as often as we could. After about six months she became well aware that I wanted to marry her. I was not shy about expressing my feelings, so when I did get around to asking her to marry me and she said yes, I thought I'd died and gone straight to heaven. She said I would need to ask her dad for his permission. She's wonderfully old-fashioned that way.

My meeting with Mac was awkward because for the previous six years we had been friends, and now I was asking him to become my father-in-law. After a brief drive in his Toyota Celica we parked in front of their house and talked for what seemed like an hour. I'll never forget what he said to me before he said yes. He said, "You will make this marriage work." Based on our lengthy discussion I knew his concerns and reservations because of my failed marriage, and I took his blunt statement to mean that failure in my marriage to Sandy was not an option.

Now, after thirty-five amazing and incredible years of marriage with Sandy, our three grown daughters are married and we have grandchildren. Every grandchild adores and loves their Grammy, as do I. My life is so much more meaningful and purposeful when I'm in Sandy's company. She is beautiful, graceful, silly, fashionable, extraordinary, and very intelligent. Every day I try to be worthy of her companionship.

On the trail, after the first stop for some refreshment (and hopefully some of Sandy's cookies), about another mile up is the second place to rest: a tree that has become known as the Lunch Tree. On one of his first hikes up the trail, Rob's dad, Franklin Glen, stopped to rest beneath a very large old western hemlock (cedar) tree. It was unique. It had survived the major fire of the 1920s. It had been much taller, but the top of the tree had been blown out by some ice and windstorms many years ago. The first limbs of the tree are at least twenty-five feet from its base, and when you look skyward at those limbs, they are over twelve inches in diameter, creating a large canopy of shade and shelter, especially during rain. The tree trunk is at least seven feet in diameter at its base, which has become partially diseased and developed a significant opening on the trail-facing side. I call it a "Winnie the Pooh, home-like entrance."

As Franklin Glen rested from his hike, he took in some nourishment and decided to leave some candy bars right at the opening in the tree. Later, when he reached the cabin, he mentioned to us that he stopped at the tree to have lunch and subsequently left some snacks for anyone who might happen by and notice them. Thus, that tree became known as the "Lunch Tree."

Over the years, Rob became fascinated with the large opening in the tree. Whenever we were hiking together we would always stop, rest, and have a snack or lunch there. Often, Rob would take out his hatchet and extricate some of the diseased wood inside. With Rob, fascination became a fixation about the great and grand Lunch Tree. Channeling some sort of internal arborist inclinations, he did whatever he could to improve the overall health of the tree. Hollowing out more of the disease seemed to make sense. Any time you can remove termites from a living tree it is a good thing.

On one solo trip up the trail, Rob decided he was going to do some major surgery on the inside of the Lunch Tree. Hatchet in hand, he crawled inside and began to perform his caregiving operation. One could literally stand up inside the tree. Rob began cleaning out the loose deadwood and diseased area around his hips and shoulders. Determined to remove all debris inside the tree, he took his hatchet and began chopping above shoulder height.

Suddenly, an avalanche of dead wood rained down, literally encasing him inside the tree. One arm was above his head, hatchet still in hand; his other arm was pinned against his hip. Panic had yet to set in because a little pocket of air surrounded his face. Yet he couldn't move his head, legs, arms, or shoulders. Seconds passed in silence. After a minute of being wrapped inside the tree as if he were in a cocoon, he started to feel a bit of worry. Tired of being in the dark and unable to move, he tried wriggling the hand down by his hip again. In one sudden moment, this tree seemed to have a contraction and he literally was birthed from the tree—he was pushed out of the opening like a baby who was born breach. Oh, how I wish someone would've walked by at that very moment; what would've been the expression on their face, seeing a grown man pushed out of a hollowed-out tree, laying on the ground in the fetal position covered with dried, rotted tree placenta?

A few years after Rob's birthing incident at the Lunch Tree, Providence did shine down upon me. Rob and I were making yet another one of our many pilgrimages to the cabin. It was in the summer, and the Nootka rose bushes had burst forth with their large pink flowers. Thimbleberry bushes were scattered along the edge of the trail in thickets. Their white flowers had bloomed; soon their edible, raspberry-like fruit would be enjoyed by bears and some humans. The same was true for the salmonberry and red huckleberry that are found in abundance in the mountains there.

When we reached the Lunch Tree, as is the tradition, we stopped and had a snack. I had comfortably seated myself on a rock when Rob walked over to the tree with his hatchet and proceeded to almost completely disappear inside. I thought to myself, *This will be interesting.* Within a matter of just a few minutes, perhaps two at the most, a chunk of cedar wood the size of a bowling ball rolled out the entrance to the tree and onto the ground. Right behind that large chunk of wood came Rob, wobbling out of the tree rubbing his head and mumbling a few obscenities. I'm sorry, but I laughed. I know I should've instantaneously said, "Rob, I'm so sorry you hit your head, are you alright?" except, that's not how our relationship has worked over the past fifty years. If he was seriously hurt, I'm sure I'd have some measure of concern and sympathy. He just couldn't leave that tree alone!

🔺

Past the infamous Lunch Tree, a beautiful cedar grove lay in wait. This grove of trees was just below an area we called "Turning the corner." Keep in mind the hike itself to the Cedar Grove keeps getting steeper and steeper, especially the long stretches without any switchbacks.

There are also several Douglas fir trees, a few bigleaf maples, and some vine maple bushes keeping the cedar trees company. Prior to the grove, the trail winds through the open part of a wooded canyon where in the spring, summer, or autumn, shrubs and bushes always assert themselves and encroach upon the trail. Here and on other parts of the hike it seems like you're walking in some part of the Amazon jungle, perhaps wishing you had a machete to hack down some of the vegetation impeding your progress.

About fifty yards before the grove, a large bigleaf maple tree used to grow on the uphill side of the trail. It had blown over in some windstorm and still had its major root system intact, along with its will to survive. This massive maple's trunk and limbs now hung out over the canyon on the downhill side of the trail. For several years it provided a wonderful place to stop and perch oneself to look back over the scenery. It provided a fantastic view of the river below and the mountains on the other side of the river. Eventually, more storms wrought havoc until that beautiful maple lost its battle and fell into the ravine.

Albert Camus wrote, "Autumn is a second spring when every leaf is a flower." In late September, all of October, and most of November, the fall foliage along the trail is at its most stunning. The leaves from many deciduous trees and shrubs explode in bright reds, golden yellows, and hints of orange. Along the trail clear up to the Cedar Grove, the big leaf maples are in abundance and their autumn leaves lay a thick carpet along the trail. The vine maples are a favorite forage plant for both deer and elk. They thrive in the trail's environment, which is well watered under the natural canopy of conifers that filters sunlight. Hiking during this time of year can be mesmerizing.

Right at the entrance to the Cedar Grove there is an abrupt switchback where the trail turns steeply to the left. During non-winter months, you literally duck under some vine maples as you enter the grove itself. I still remember the first time I saw this grove of trees. The cedars themselves stood apart from the Douglas firs as great

sentinels terracing the hillside above. On any day there's a notice-
able temperature change as you enter the grove, and especially on a
hot summer day the temperature will drop at least 10 degrees.

In the springtime, summer, and autumn whenever I've entered the
Cedar Grove over the past forty-five years, I almost always pause
and look around—making an accounting of these great cedar trees
and how they've endured for decades, especially the nearly five
decades I've known them.

On the other hand, whenever I've approached the Cedar Grove
in winter, I've already hiked nearly three miles and that part of
the journey to the cabin has been either very wet, icy, or both. The
winter weather on hikes to the cabin varies, but one consistent
thing is that gray clouds usually keep the sun hidden. You rarely
see any blue skies from December to March. When the ground is
icy, the trail becomes especially treacherous and needs to be taken
slowly. Fog can obscure the light and it is hard to find toeholds
along the edge of the trail. Because it's difficult to walk directly
on the trail, you must do your best to kick toeholds on either side
or crawl through the brush by cutting switchbacks. Sometimes, we
used sharpened sticks as walking staffs to help with balance on the
ice, and for breaking toeholds in the dirt. On certain stretches we
crawled along on all fours, as this was the only way to advance
along the trail. Hiking the trail in the winter, especially after an ice
storm, is exhausting and dangerous work.

🌲

When you get to the Cedar Grove and "turn the corner," you climb
in elevation through the old growth forest for perhaps half a mile,
until the trail meanders through a small, rocky, open area where
a few vine maple and huckleberry bushes politely inform human
visitors, If you pass on by you will discover that the trail will be
friendly and welcoming; no more steep climbs to struggle with,

nor rock slides to scramble over or around, nor cliffs to possibly slip and fall off. The place to "jump off the trail" is right past a tiny spring, running year-round, which carved its way across the trail. From there, the bushwhacking begins.

For several years I'd yearned to hike the trail again, to find the Big Cedar Tree once more and hike farther on to see the cabin Rob had told me so much about. When I beheld the cabin for the first time, I was amazed at how hard it was to see among the dense forest vegetation. That seemed like a good thing to me. The cedar shake roof stood out in contrast to the weathered walls of the cabin. The porch was sturdy, and the cabin door looked solid enough to probably keep out bear-like invaders. The first night sleeping in the cabin I was cozy and warm, but was awakened by the sounds of the cabin creaking. Apparently several standing trees rub up against the cabin roof when the wind blows hard enough. That sound took some getting used to. This place would be my preferred wilderness Mecca. It looked built to last. Rob had accomplished something significant.

Chapter 7
Pentathlons in the Wilderness

"The most important thing in the Olympic games is not winning but taking part; the essential thing in life is not conquering but fighting well." —Pierre de Coubertin

The Bull of the Woods Pentathlon is an informal gathering of friends held at the cabin, usually in late August. Rob would probably say the ostensible reasons for this event are to ensure we returned up the trail at least once each year, to encourage regular fitness, and to provide a benchmark for our capability to develop our individual wilderness skills and prowess as the years pass and we age.

The five "official" events are:

1. Logging (sawing, chopping, splitting, stacking)
2. Fire building
3. Marksmanship
4. Orienteering
5. Swimming

However, the real events are:

1. Watching each other attempt to get lost in the woods
2. Cheering fellow participants to not give up
3. Debating rules infractions just because we like to debate
4. Making creative excuses for our individual poor performances
5. Getting away from civilization to spend time with each other as friends

✦

Both Rob and I lived in California in late 1985. He lived in Livermore, while Sandy and I lived in Modesto. We communicated on a regular basis, and hatched the pentathlon idea for the summer of 1986; we wanted to share the entire ambience of the cabin with selected friends and family. I was in charge of marketing the event and recruiting participants. Rob was in charge of devising the handicapped scoring system and the rules associated with each event. It was decided early on that we needed more than just four of us up at the cabin running around in the woods making fools of ourselves. So, Rob invited his dad, Franklin Glen, and his only brother, Brad.

As I contemplated who else to invite to our inaugural pentathlon, my old friend Mike crossed my mind. I thought he might like to join us even though we had lost touch. I sent him an invitation to join us up in the mountains at the cabin for the pentathlon, and he accepted.

I asked Mike why he accepted the invitation, since it had been a long time since he'd seen Rob or me, and he said he realized that all he basically did in his personal life was work. He was involved in the family business, which consumed a lot of his time. He would take time off work to exercise, and climbed stairs a lot to try to get in shape, but he liked the idea of setting goals and having plans. looked at maps of the terrain. He thought it would be fun.

On July 23, 1986, I mailed out the invitations. They were full of hype. I started off by mentioning the Goodwill Games, which had ended, and how it was time for the "real" games to begin on August 30th, 1986. I invoked the following quotation from *Jeremiah Johnson*:

> *"Many a man has journeyed to the mountains to get from nature, something nature couldn't give him below. Mountain's got its own way, pilgrim." -Bear Claw.*

I attempted to flatter every invitee enough to believe that even receiving an invitation to such an extraordinary event was an honor. My letter was written to appeal to a certain ego that existed with all of us back in 1985–1986. We were all very competitive individuals, and we each seemed to derive a certain amount of satisfaction from the idea of seeing each other compete in things that we were really not very capable of doing; of course, we also wanted to ultimately discover who might actually win this oddly contrived wilderness spectacle and receive the ultimate prize, the silver chalice.

Participants were required to sign and return their RSVP no later than August 8th. Things got even sillier when I attached a single page titled "Comments and Notes." It was filled with more bluster and bravado. My marketing efforts worked—we had 100 percent attendance in 1986. The participants were Rob, Franklin Glen, Brad, Mike, Dave, and myself. There was only one nonparticipant to attend our inaugural wilderness pentathlon, Sandy, who was to serve as scorekeeper, judge if needed, and, of course, provide homemade cookies.

I can hear Rob saying, "Not true, John, this pentathlon is only about getting together up at the cabin as friends and family, enjoying each other's company." Mike might have feigned a similar response, never admitting publicly or privately that competition between us was the driving reason for participation.

Brad would write in the guestbook after our first Pentathlon that, "The cabin has been on my mind since I first went to the lean-to. This trip has been the greatest yet: good competition, great company and more importantly good food."[10]

Dave always put forth his best effort in sporting events. Yet, he always tried to act like he wasn't competitive. He recorded, "Up with Brad (started up the trail at 7:30 PM arrived at the cabin at 10:30 PM). Pentathlon competition Saturday, rain Friday, Saturday & Sunday, lots of fun, good food, swimming. Sandy was terrific. Dave #50."[10]

Included in the invitation packet was Rob's comprehensive six-page explanation of the rules for every event. Rob's remarkable math aptitude and intellect allowed him to carefully calculate an intricate handicap and scoring system, so that all participants would be on equal footing regardless of age or the event. Someone who might be sixty-five years old would not have a disadvantage competing against someone who was, say, eighteen years old. In other words, there were handicaps afforded to older folks. In 1986 the youngest participant (Brad) was about twenty-five years old. His father Franklin Glen was sixty-two; the rest of us were between thirty-three and thirty-seven years old.

On the Friday before the Pentathlon, Mike, Sandy, and I arrived at the cabin around 6 p.m. It was a beautiful summer day, warm and pleasant. Rob and FGB (Franklin Glen) arrived a little after 8p.m. We had a fine dinner and then waited for Dave and Brad to show. After waiting longer than expected, Rob went looking for them at about 10 p.m., flashlight in hand.

Dave and Brad ushered in the first Wilderness Pentathlon at the cabin by hiking the last half of the trail in the dark without moon-light or a flashlight. There was plenty of light when they headed out of the parking lot, but an hour into the hike it became completely pitch black. They couldn't tell the difference when their eyes were closed or open. To make things more exciting, they were on the steepest part of the trail. Brad knew their matches weren't going to last long, and tried burning a little piece of paper or two. Standing within just a few feet from each other in total darkness, they were talking about their options when Dave had the clever idea to burn his spare socks wrapped around a stick, using them as a torch to light the way. Unfortunately, a sock doesn't last long when it's on fire. Once the first one was burnt down to ashes, Dave reached into his pack, pulled out another one, and repeated the procedure. The socks were not 100 percent cotton and smoked profusely with a pungent odor. Brad was hiking close behind Dave in order to see, and was nearly asphyxiated by the noxious black smoke emitting from Dave's white socks.

Neither was worried, but they didn't want to use all of their socks and figured they would just sleep on the trail. They were just getting settled for the night when they saw a light farther up the trail. Rob had come to find them, and his flashlight illuminated that they had stopped precariously close to a rocky drop-off along the trail. They finally made it to the jump-off point and the cabin, mostly thanks to Rob.

Back then, our small Jeremiah Johnson-style cabin could only accommodate two people inside comfortably. Two more people could sleep on the porch without crowding each other. There's a nice level spot just off the porch where folks could set up a couple of small tents or canopies to stay out of the rain if needed. After Brad and Dave arrived, they got the last of the spaghetti dinner, salad, and French bread. In between bites of dinner they told their version of hiking up the trail. To this day, Brad can tell you a fabulous yarn about how bad it was hiking behind Dave and breathing those toxic fumes from his spare socks. Little by little, everyone said good-night and left the outdoor campfire to sleep in their "staked-out" sleeping areas not far from the cabin. Franklin Glen slept inside and snored like a hibernating bear.

Saturday morning broke with intermittent, drizzling rain. The ground was damp with a chill in the air. Dave was up early and had a nice cooking fire going in the outdoor fire pit. A light breakfast was available beginning at 7:15 a.m. The games themselves would begin at 10 a.m. Predictably, there was plenty of hot water for the coffee and hot chocolate drinkers. No one seemed to be in a big rush to begin this wilderness pentathlon. We'd hoped that the temperature would be in the high 70s or 80s. Instead, it never reached 60 degrees.

As we sat around our warm fire with a copy of the rules in front of us, Rob took charge, explaining all the details about each of the five events. Contestants need not enter all events to win. The mathematically challenged of us needed further explanation that the scoring of the pentathlon was on a decaying exponential curve. That meant there was a maximum (theoretical) score for each event, but no minimum score.

Despite Rob's thorough explanation, there was some uncertainty or apprehension as we prepared for the logging contest. I chose to simply give my best efforts during the competition itself and see how things worked out.

⁂

Logging/Wood Cutting was a timed event consisting of four tasks: sawing, chopping, splitting, and stacking. The stopwatch would run continuously. A single cedar log, fifteen to sixteen inches across the smallest diameter, was used for the sawing. Each contestant would cut a single round (two to three inches thick) and continue immediately to the chopping task. A single fir log was to be used for chopping. Each contestant was to chop through the log one time to obtain a single round twenty inches long on the bottom side. The round must then be split into eight pieces of firewood, which must be of roughly equal size. The watch would stop when the eight pieces of firewood were stacked neatly.

We each took turns using the one-man crosscut saw that had been up at the cabin since its inception. There's an art to using a crosscut saw. When my turn came, I made one cut into the cedar log, being sure that the slice was at least two inches thick. In order for me to proceed to the wood-chopping portion of the logging event, I needed to get that cedar "round" cut quickly. By the time I cut through the log I was completely winded.

I grabbed my axe and ran quickly to the prescribed chopping area where a Douglas fir log, (long since dead) was purposefully wedged barely above the ground; ready to be chopped into a 20-inch length. The log itself was just over ten inches in diameter. The rules stated that the log needed to be chopped through with the axe without changing sides or rotating the log.

I've chopped my fair share of firewood over the years and thought I'd be pretty good at this event. However, using the cross-cut saw spent a lot of my energy. In my mind I could hear the clock ticking, and every second meant fewer points I would earn in this event. With every swing and whack of the axe, chips of wood exploded away from the log. I was making progress. Soon my arms felt like rubber and the force behind my chopping grew weaker. Several blows just bounced off the log. My peers could see me struggling and offered some words of encouragement.

I had to stop and catch my breath before I could proceed any further. Finally, the log I was chopping separated, and the required 20-inch section lay on the ground, ready to be split and stacked. My arms were so mushy that the splitting of the log into the required pieces took too much time. The stopwatch stopped when I stacked the final piece of wood as required. My spectator friends offered their kudos as I stood there limply holding the axe, recognizing my pathetic effort.

When the scores were tallied for that single event, Dave crushed everyone (to no one's surprise). He was a beast when it came to the logging event.

Fire building was the second event in the pentathlon. It was a timed event requiring each participant to build a fire from scratch on the ground, large enough to burn through a cotton string stretched between two "posts" twenty-four inches above the ground. The only equipment allowed is an axe or hatchet, a knife, and one single wooden match. Only the wood materials produced during the logging competition are to be used as fuel. These materials include the cedar round and the fir pieces split after chopping. Each contestant must use his or her own wood from the logging competition. If a contestant did not enter or complete the logging, equivalent materials were provided. At the GO signal, all contestants had exactly ten minutes to prepare their fuel. After ten minutes, the stopwatch for the event started and all contestants were timed simultaneously. Each contestant was responsible for watching his string and notifying the time keeper when it had broken as a result of the fire. Extra matches were available for a two-minute penalty per match requested.

To be a successful fire builder requires a tremendous amount of skill and a certain amount of luck. If you were a spectator watching this event, you would see all the participants in close proximity to each other huddled over their piles of unprepared, natural wood. Each would be within a few feet of their assigned fire-building station. They would be using either their axe, hatchet, and/or knife to fashion the perfect combination of "kindling" necessary to generate a combustible fire.

Every contestant was preoccupied with creating and amassing their perfect amount of fire material; then, when Sandy shouted "GO," every fire builder was jolted into action and they grabbed their fire materials and began placing small portions of tinder on the ground below their respective cotton strings.

One never knew exactly how the fire building would go. Suddenly you would hear the sound of wood combusting and glance to another contestant, realizing their one match had ignited their prepared burnable material, their face within inches of the tiny flame as they fanned it with their breath. Looking peripherally, you would see other contestant's fire growing slowly. One fire may have flames burning around the cotton string but not burning through. Another fire may just be billowing smoke. When a fire builder shouted, "My string is burnt through," the fire judge acknowledged that fact and recorded their time.

Each Pentathlon fire-building champion has had four things in common. Each carefully prepared their fire materials and was reasonably certain they had the right amount of wood shavings, cedar tinder, and other fire material available to combust before they struck their "one" match. No champion ever used more than one match. Every champion had a knack for patiently placing their kindling and other sticks on their fire so they never smothered the flame. Terry, who would join the festivities for our second pentathlon, typically won the fire-building event. At its conclusion, the fire-building competition area was carefully cleared and all the small fires were totally extinguished. I usually would be the last or nearly last person to complete this event, and Dave came away with the fire-building victory in 1986.

Marksmanship / Target Shooting was always the next event. The rules stated that a small caliber pistol was allowable (rim or pellet fire). Rob provided a .777 caliber target air gun. This event allowed for two practice rounds shooting at a standard NRA slow fire pistol target fifty feet away. One must shoot standing, holding the gun (freehand) either using one or both hands. Five shots per target, recording the best score of the two.

This event always took more time than planned because every participant would shoot once at the target, walk to the target and examine and analyze where their shot hit or missed, and then walk back the required fifty feet from the target and do so nine more times. Also, some fellow competitors and spectators would talk a little trash, hoping to rattle their opponents.

Rob dominated this event in most every pentathlon contest. The reason is simple. He owned the target pistol, and he practiced.

⋀

Orienteering is a competitive sport in which participants find their way to various checkpoints across rough country with the aid of a map and compass, the winner being the one with the lowest elapsed time.

Rob, Dave, Mike, and myself were in our prime in 1986 when the pentathlon concept was conceived, and Rob and I discussed that it might be motivating to design one event to be the most challenging physically, emotionally, and mentally—orienteering became that event. Due to the thick vegetation in this area of the forest, if you began hiking from any corner of the cabin through the woods for even less than a half mile without a map, compass, or landmark, you needed exceptional orienting skills or you would get lost.

After doing some research about orienteering and its history, I think some of Rob's ancestral DNA could be part of the reason he actually likes tramping through the woods. The history of orienteering began in the late 19th century in Sweden; the actual term "orientering" was first used in 1886 and meant the crossing of unknown land with the aid of a map and a compass. In Sweden, orienteering grew from military training in land navigation into a competitive sport for military officers, then for civilians. Rob's grandfather, Erik, was born in Sweden and immigrated to the United States in the early 1900s.

Keep in mind, it wasn't until May of 1989 that the first consumer handheld GPS device was available commercially. The device weighed less than two pounds and was waterproof and floatable. It looked like a large calculator and featured a display screen powered by six AA batteries. It sold for $3,000 and was called the Magellan GPS, named after Ferdinand Magellan, who was the first person to circumnavigate the Earth.

The orienteering route Rob chose was not complex—we just needed to travel south, southwest to the highest peak marked on the topographical map we were given before the orienteering event began. At that summit was a cache of wristbands. We were instructed to take one and then find our way back to the cabin.

We were all required to take a compass, whistle, the topographical map, and some additional emergency items should we get lost. We all knew this particular course would be 85 percent bushwhacking and 15 percent trail. None of us knew exactly how long it might take, except perhaps Rob. In my letter of invitation to all the participants I stated in bold lettering, "Any individual complaining about the starting order will be assessed fifteen minutes to their accumulative time." Additionally, I stated that the infamous Dave (who claims to hold the unofficial record of fifty-six minutes for running from the bottom of the trail to the cabin) would leave at the same time with Rob, ten minutes after Brad, Mike, and I departed. When the clock started to keep track of each person's time to complete the orienteering event, Franklin Glen was the first to leave. Since he was the senior citizen of the group, he left twenty-seven minutes ahead of Brad, Mike, and myself. After Brad, Mike, and I were given the green light to begin our orienteering through the woods to the summit of a peak less than two miles away, we lost track of each other within the first hundred yards.

The topographical map had a lot of detail about the terrain. I knew from experience that I could travel due south for about two-thirds of a mile, and if my heading was right I could avoid a lot of vine maple and other brushy areas. Within a third of a mile after leaving the cabin, I crossed another trail running east and west, but I chose to stay on my direct line compass heading. Before proceeding farther south and leaving that trail behind, I stopped and tied a small strip of red plastic that I brought with me to the limb of a 7-foot Douglas fir tree.

My biggest challenges were to slow down enough, make sure to check my compass heading using the topographical map, and avoid getting off course and missing the summit where the wristbands were placed. The summit was surrounded by dense forest and only at the very top was a small pile of rocks. I finally reached the summit, and two wristbands were gone. I wondered who had been there already but quickly headed back by a different route.

I got a little disoriented and off course, and when I finally arrived at the cabin, both Mike and Rob were there. Astonishingly, Mike had been back for over an hour and a half. When asked about his orienteering success, he remarked that it was really no secret. He went up there multiple times before the pentathlon and decided on what he thought would be the best route, then stuck to his plan. Mike doesn't get riled up very easily, staying calm and focused.

Rob had arrived just a little over thirty minutes before me. Soon enough, Dave and Franklin Glen arrived seconds apart from each other. They must have crossed paths and decided to walk in together from that point. Brad was a few minutes behind them. It was a great cause for celebration. No one had gotten lost, and each had their stories to tell about their trek through the woods.

Swimming was the last event, presenting one of our more physical challenges. High mountain lakes in late August, mid-September, or perhaps early October can be a little chilly. Originally, the swimming event was to be about 400 yards in total distance. Swim out 200 yards, grab a wristband, then swim 200 yards back. For the first two pentathlons, that was the case. The swim course was shortened to about 200 yards in 1988. The decision to make that change resulted from whining and complaining by some people, including myself, for having to swim so far.

The initial rules stated the highest scorers in the first four events would swim first. In 1986, that meant I would swim third. I dove into the water and resolved to swim as fast as I could. What did I have to lose? The silver chalice was out of my reach and I was in third place. None of us had trained for the swimming event. It was late afternoon and all of us looked a little spent from our orienteering experience; at least, I was. I tried to use my finest swimming technique, thinking it would pay off. The only time I looked up was to make sure I wasn't swimming in a meandering fashion. When I finally reached the prescribed spot, I quickly reached up and grabbed a wristband then began swimming frantically for the finish. Fatigue was beginning to take its toll on me. I pressed forward, taking many more breaths of air than in the first 200 yards. Reaching the finish, I hauled myself out of the water in order for the timekeeper's clock to stop. My time was respectable. Dave had yet to swim, and if anyone could beat my time it would've been him. Remarkably, my time held and I surprisingly won the swimming event!

⟁

The first wilderness pentathlon was over, with Mike, easygoing smile intact, emerging as the victor. It probably had a lot to do with the fact that he was very pragmatic and had diligently strategized how to do well up in the mountains. It was now time to celebrate and commiserate around the big campfire while feasting upon a fabulous dinner. The steaks were cooked, as were the baked potatoes. The green salad was fresh and the rice pilaf was cooked to perfection. The corn on the cob was delicious. Rob and Dave had carried watermelons up the trail to the cabin. I like to think we pioneered the concept of being wilderness foodies and prided ourselves on our non-backpacking food.

Of course, there were plenty of Sandy's cowgirl cookies to go around. I know for a fact that most people like nuts in their cookies and I just happen to be in the minority who doesn't. My favorite cookie ingredients include raisins, oatmeal, chocolate chips, and all the other important ingredients that go into making it a delicious cookie—except nuts! A few days before leaving on any trip to the cabin I'd say to Sandy, "Sweet Sandy, I'm planning a trip to the cabin, can you make me some cowboy cookies?" She'd always make a double batch, and it wasn't until a few years ago that our daughter Emily pointed out it didn't make much sense to call my favorite cookie a "cowboy cookie," particularly because it didn't contain any nuts. So, appropriately, we began calling them cowgirl cookies.

There was plenty of firewood left over from the fire-building competition to keep our bonfire blazing. Over the next several hours, each of us reveled in each other's company. Rob's dad, Franklin Glen, seemed gratified that he was included and that he had shared this experience with his two sons.

Sandy, the camp queen, brought us all good luck. Her beaming smiles and words of encouragement motivated each of us to enjoy being in the moment. I was the luckiest man there to have her sitting next to me. As I glanced around the campfire I saw the various silhouetted faces of my friends, each looking totally content in the camaraderie and bond of friendship that was created by being at the cabin. This was a joyous occasion never to be forgotten.

For three consecutive years we held our wilderness pentathlons. In 1987, we invited a few more people to participate: Mac, Rob's friend Carol, and Terry. Mac was a willing participant, as he was always game to participate in an athletic event and the pentathlon was a good excuse for him to come see the cabin he had heard so much about.

After our missions, Terry and I had lost track of each other living in different places, but he had moved to Oregon to attend dental school from 1982–1987. I had moved to the Portland area with Sandy and our three daughters in November of 1985. Terry, too, had married, and he and his wife Laraine had three children as well. We had kept in touch a little bit via mail, but we truly reconnected in 1986. It was really a great reunion. He hadn't changed much, except for looking a bit older, but he was the same bright-eyed, enthusiastic guy I knew back in New Orleans. Our reunion was easy—it was almost like ten years never passed. That's the way it is with Terry; he's just engaging and likable. With his excellent outdoor woodsman skills, he was a great addition to the cabin circle of friends.

Carol, Terry, and Mac all made a good showing, but to no one's surprise, Dave won the 1987 silver chalice. He placed first or second in four of the five events. The big surprise that year was Brad getting lost orienteering. He had done well in the earlier events and was satisfied with his performance thus far. In his words, the orienteering seemed "pretty damn simple." Once he got pretty far out from the start, he realized he was going around in a circle. It was getting dark, and he just kept hiking without seeming to get anywhere. He wasn't worried because it wasn't that cold, but finally he decided he didn't want to hike in the dark. He found a spot on the edge of the trail and decided to camp out there; in the morning he would try to find his way back to the cabin. He built a fire and was planning to stoke it as best he could and sleep close to it. Suddenly he heard me, Mike, Dave, and Rob calling his name. He called back to us and when we found him sitting by the trail he had a really nice fire going. He casually greeted us, not sounding the least bit worried at all. "Glad you happened by, I was getting lonely. Before you showed up I'd been thinking about the nice steak dinner waiting for me back at the cabin. It's still waiting for me, right?"

We laughed, and Rob said, "John and Dave were thinking of cooking your steak and eating it as payment for coming and finding you. I talked them out of that idea."

Chuckling, Brad replied, "Rob, I always knew you were my favorite brother." We helped Brad put his trailside fire out and returned to the cabin. Brad getting lost, along with some suggestions from those in attendance, resulted in the original pentathlon rules being modified to accommodate more women, aging men, and ways the orienteering event might be improved.

🜨

In 1988, Franklin Glen won the silver chalice at age sixty-four. The scoring in the handicap system seemed to be working. Glen improved dramatically in the logging, orienteering, and swimming events. It was a well-deserved victory. I'm not exactly sure why, but it was decided we'd take a pentathlon sabbatical, making it a less frequent occurrence.

I moved away with my family and lived in eastern Oregon from December 1988 until June 1992, when we moved to Idaho. Other than Glen and Mac, who were retiring or nearing retirement, the rest of us were settling into our work world, raising our families and spending most of our time with them. Our trips to the cabin began to dwindle. Twelve years later, in September 2000, another wilderness pentathlon took place. Dave brought his son Jacob. Rob, Dave, Terry, and I were the only other participants. This event was unique because, for the first time, another generation was participating. Rob became the proud owner of a silver chalice that year. He didn't hold back as he might have during previous competitions.

In 2002, we gave the pentathlon another try. Rob modified the pentathlon rules a little bit again. He stated, "Among other things, there will be a fishing option to the orienteering course! This event is not timed. Scores will be based on the longest fish: One hundred points per inch with possible compensation for agedness. Teams of two are encouraged. We'll figure out how to score the teams later. . ." In addition to those changes, Rob used some new form of calculus and averaging methods, which resulted in me becoming the overall champion. Yes, I had been the most improved from the previous four pentathlons compared to the other pentathletes, but it didn't seem like an outright victory to me. Everyone who had competed seemed pleased that I would claim the prized silver chalice. They were gracious about the end result.

Two more wilderness pentathlons occurred in 2003 and 2008. Impressively, Mac won the silver chalice in 2003 at the age of seventy-one. That was the year I introduced my ninja shorty wetsuit for the swim event. I was mocked endlessly for such a brazen act of stretching the rules.

In 2008, Dave's son Jacob brought his friends Bob and Austin. Our daughter Desirae, her husband Kevin, and our friend Wade were new challengers for the silver chalice. When you added Rob, Mac, Dave, Terry, and myself, that made twelve contestants. It was a big crowd. It seemed with each pentathlon Rob, Mike, Terry, Dave, and I became a little closer as friends. We all respected each other's differences and rejoiced in what we had in common.

In some cases the two-team method was adopted. Mac, age seventy-six, and Desirae, age twenty-seven, combined efforts. Kevin, a total newbie to the area and the cabin, became my teammate. He went with me on the orienteering event and we arrived at the infamous mountain peak where the required wristbands waited to be retrieved. When we arrived all the wristbands were there, meaning no one else had been there yet. Surprised, we grabbed our wristbands and headed toward the lake where other wristbands needed to be recovered. Thoughts of winning the orienteering competition floated through my mind. Kevin in tow, I began making my way down to the lake as rapidly as possible.

We were in a more wide-open area of the forest where very little windfall lay on the ground, which made for faster travel. Since leaving the summit, we'd been bushwhacking about ten to fifteen minutes when, not too far off in the distance, we heard a sound we didn't recognize. We stopped, crouched down, and began scanning the forest so that we might see what kind of animal was making such a racket. I'd never heard such a strange sound before in the woods. Was it an elk running through the forest gasping for air, fleeing from some predator? Could it be a black bear chasing after some prey? My heart began to race as I scanned the area to see what creature may have been getting closer and louder.

Suddenly, about a hundred yards away from where we were hidden, running uphill as fast as he could—was Rob. He was bellowing a loud *whoa* sound, something a huge barking dog might make. Confused, we watched him continue to run up the hillside making his strange sound. I remarked, "Kevin, let's go. Rob is behaving like a crazy man right now. This might be our chance to win the orienteering. We'll get our wristbands at the lake before he reaches the cache up on top of the peak. That's where he's clearly headed." Shaking his head, Kevin replied, "Ready when you are, John."

Pushing aside that distraction, we hustled our way down to the lake, grabbed our wristbands, and charted the quickest route back to the cabin. When we arrived, to *our* surprise Rob was already there. We questioned him about his earlier antics, and he told us that as he was orienteering up the hill from the lake, he came upon a recently killed deer. The predator that killed it (probably a bear) had left its prey because of the noise Rob had been making while tramping through the woods. Suddenly, it dawned on Rob that whatever the predator was, might not like the fact that he was standing over its dinner and might return unexpectedly asking him to leave in no uncertain terms. Not wanting to be asked to leave, Rob departed running like hell, hoping he could make a louder and much scarier sound so that his real, or imagined, bear might not suddenly appear thinking Rob might make an excellent dessert.

Due to the age handicap and fishing option, Desirae and Mac won the silver chalice in 2008. We all had a great time. We missed Mike, Dave, and Terry, who did not attend.

On seven occasions spanning a twenty-year period of time, friends would gather around a post-pentathlon campfire to celebrate. Memories were made, and every pentathlon campfire cast off some night light and warmth, allowing each of us to see the silhouetted faces of our friends and their individual facial expressions captured as another memory because they, like myself, were in the mountains near a tiny, irreplaceable cabin that welcomed all who came to visit.

Chapter 8

Time Marches On, Invaders Come & Go, Things Change

"You can't go back and change the beginning, but you can start where you are and change the ending." —C.S. Lewis

When the cabin was being built in 1979, it seemed uninvited, like it didn't belong there. Gradually over time, the cabin blended in with the forest and almost became one with the habitat it shared. However, it wasn't fully camouflaged—it saw its fair share of invaders over the years.

Black bears were the first to assault the cabin. One fall, Dave found the cabin in shambles. Bears had ripped off the door and helped themselves to everything. The Shepard's stove was smashed, and all food was destroyed. Most everything else had been thrown outside: clothes, bags, etc.

Rob was not with Dave, but later recorded, "Judging from the damage, the bear, or bears, simply chewed into the cedar until it could get a purchase with its teeth, and then just kept pulling outward. Eventually the door broke in half, with the right half still swinging on the hinges, the left half with the latch lying on the ground. To break the door in half they had to pull out over a dozen 20d nails, which would take incredible strength."

The bears dragged everything outside except the tools. The sleeping bags and books were soaking wet and ruined. Clearly, they didn't want any of these items. Rob was convinced that the bear, or bears, hauled all the nonedible items outside just to annoy him. All the food was also gone, including anything in glass bottles. Every bottle (ketchup, etc.) had the cap removed. None of the bottles were broken, yet all the contents were gone. They looked like they'd been through a dishwasher. Pretty neat trick! Among the empties included a bottle of whiskey, which had been full. Near the empty whiskey bottle, Dave found several patches of bear hide with black fur. The bears must have gotten drunk and had some disagreement about who got what. Damn bears!

Repairs were made to the destruction and greater fortifications were built to thwart possible future attacks. After the bear attacks, a more stealth invasion occurred. Our new enemies were mice, packrats, and one rogue-snarling R.O.U.S.[11] The mice and packrats tormented us. Dave was first to bravely fight off our new enemies' invasions by filling in all the open cracks and spaces in the cabin logs with some special foam insulation, dispensed from pressurized canisters.

Now a no-tolerance policy with the mice and their much larger friends, packrats, was enforced. The wood rats would make parts of the cabin their home in our absence. For several years, they staked their claim with nests up in the eves and defecating inside the cabin, making our visits very unpleasant.

The war waged on, and our enemies seemed to be winning. Our visits to the cabin were too infrequent, and the mice always seemed to multiply in our absence. Every cabin built in remote mountain areas has mice. Putting out a few traps and managing the problem is an option. However, managing problems is mostly what governments and poorly run businesses generally do. Our approach was to solve the problem by winning enough battles with our enemies that they would retreat (go somewhere else) for at least several years.

One battle tactic to outmaneuver the mice was to raise the cabin higher off the ground so those pesky pests could no longer build their nests underneath. The initial plan was to use a very long log and three fat men as a lever to lift the corners of the cabin higher; that plan was tried and abandoned. Instead, Rob hauled up two 5-ton hydraulic jacks to get the job done. It took both jacks positioned carefully on each side of one corner of the cabin to get the cabin raised to the desired height. As the cabin was being raised it moaned as if it were in some sort of pain. Rob crawled underneath the cabin and moved rocks into their necessary positions, all the while hoping the jacks would not fail.

Mike brought up a gun to implement Rob's new "shoot the (rat) invaders onsite" policy. The rats were fearless. Several were dispatched outside, but Mike and Rob also executed several inside. The holes were visible in the cedar paneling for years afterwards. Rob squished one behind the woodpile and smacked another one virtually out of the air with an axe handle.

An additional cross layer of boards was added to the floor of the cabin; this layer included some mouse-proof wire placed between the original floorboards and the new ones. Between the wire barrier, poison, and caulking, eventually the rats were thinned out to the point that they entered retreat. Some mice would still get in, but they did minimal damage and their number was kept under control with mousetraps and peanut butter.

In 1983, Rob built the finest outdoor latrine imaginable about fifty yards away from the cabin. It wasn't a traditional outhouse with three walls and door. It was a pit latrine, a very nice one. As you left the cabin and stepped off the porch facing south, you faced a couple of options. If you went straight you would see a path to take you down to the lake, which was only a hundred yards away. Just before you took that path, there was a smaller path to your left, which led to our refreshing, open-air outhouse. Yes—I said open-air. The path was lined with huckleberry bushes and ferns of both the Western Maidenhair and Deer Fern variety. That path ended at two Douglas fir trees. In between them was a unique bench made of cedar wood with a special backrest. There was an open space where the cedar bench ended; as you sat and let your derrière hang over the opening provided, you let your back, "rest," against the cedar. No need to worry about being seen while using this outdoor privy, it was far enough away from the cabin that you couldn't be seen. In the winter it was more difficult to use the infamous outhouse. I've been up at the cabin in the winter and had to shovel snow just to be able to use it.

Latrine

⋀

Changes were a good thing. A plan to make the cabin even more welcoming was started shortly after the first pentathlon. After much discussion and my prodding, all agreed that the old cabin needed renovation. From September 1986–1989 we worked to remodel the cabin. According to Rob, ". . .in a fit of recklessness we ripped off the old roof to start the process, which ended up committing us to two full years of hard labor to put it back together again." He went on to say, "In John's defense, the old cabin was not very inviting. It looked cute with its low, flat roof, but the low angle of the roof was prone to decay and the cabin had a distinctly cave-like feel. It was dark and gloomy, a little claustrophobic."

It was agreed that the foundation needed some work as well. Throughout the fall and winter of 1987, we pulled off the roof, saving the good shakes and the old roof rafters, which were to be used on the future front porch roof. Salvaging the existing shingles from the roof took time. When the original cabin roofing took place and the handmade shingles were secured, Rob and Dave had used galvanized nails. Now, in order to remove the existing shingles and preserve them for reuse, we had to slowly pry up those nails to prevent the shingles from splitting. This was a laborious chore—cedar shingles, by their very nature, tend to split easily.

Whenever the cabin principals were together, either at the cabin or elsewhere, we seemed to find time to discuss making possible changes to the cabin. At times when we (Rob, Dave, Mike, Terry, and myself) were either sitting around the nice outdoor campfire or inside the cabin, a suggestion for improving things would be proposed. We were not discontent with the cabin; our vision was more about wanting to make some improvements that would motivate each of us to return more often. Who wouldn't want to sit in a cedar-lined sauna situated in the middle of the wilderness adjacent to a small cabin? There were even discussions about a stream-fed hot tub being built.

The Cabin

During those discussions I observed that Dave didn't voice his opinion and I concluded he must have decided that his contributions to the cabin were sufficient. It didn't seem to matter to him what cabin changes might occur in the future. He knew, as we did, his cabin contributions were substantial; he was the one other person who worked with Rob to build the original cabin before it was remodeled. Regardless, Dave often contributed labor to our remodeling efforts.

The new cedar "floorboards" for the project came from bolts of wood that had been blown over by some long-ago windstorm. These cedar bolts were at most three feet in diameter. They were not the prime middle section of the tree—they usually came from sections where the branches were, and too often the grain of the wood did not run perfectly straight and true. Yet these bolts were usable if you knew how to read the wood and visualize its inner structure; Rob became very adept at making boards from such bolts of cedar.

Rob was ingenious about laying out the new floor pattern. It was a modified parquet design, and each cedar board was split to fit exactly where needed. The wood grains ran in the precise direction to sweep things out the door, and the double-layered floor prevented mice from entering from under the cabin.

One of the raging debates surrounding the remodel was the size of the cabin. After he and Terry finished the floor reconstruction, Rob added four more logs to the top of the existing walls, which made room for a loft and a taller door entry. That additional two feet of wall height made a big difference.

Eventually, the entire roof was framed with a new ridgepole. During those first few months of labor (before winter set in), Rob, Mike, and I shingled the porch roof and the front side of the cabin roof with the salvaged shingles. We covered the top and the backside of the roof with a tarp until we could finish the roof the following summer.

✣

The day after Christmas in 1986, Rob and I decided to build a sofa bed so people could sleep under the loft, off the floor of the cabin. In the past we would sleep on the floor; that would no longer be necessary, unless of course someone needed to crowd in.

There was a certain period where Mike worked a lot by himself at the cabin: building the porch, adding boxes under the bunk beds, and putting a fancy lock/slider on the door. He didn't talk to anyone about the lock, but he had the ability to make metal things at his business, so he just made it out of scrap metal and took it up to the cabin and installed it. Around this time, he and Rob redid the porch roof. Mike purchased the roof metal in Portland. He hauled up half of the powder-coated brown steel, and Rob hauled up the other half—two forty- or fifty-pound coils.

In February of 1987, Mike and I hiked up to work around the cabin. We finished the sofa bed. We remounted the stove on the floor, making it level, and split some cedar logs and shakes for the future sauna. With every major project proposed at the cabin, there would be great debate among the cabin interior and exterior architectural committee members. Rob always brought thoughtful analysis, and I could be relied upon to contribute a healthy dose of emotion to the conversation. The reconstruction continued after our 1987 pentathlon, when two skylights were added. The remaining shingling was completed. The triangular opening in the southeast gable of the new cabin roofline was not enclosed for several months. First the required plexiglass needed to be hauled up the four-mile journey. Sherpa Mike or Rob had yet to make that trek. In the meantime, the cabin was in use through the remaining months of autumn, and through the winter of 1987–88.

On one trip to the cabin, Mike had just passed the large rock boulder that we normally traversed past on our way to the Big Cedar Tree. He stopped briefly and picked up a flat rock the size of a small dinner plate. Back at the cabin, he took a chisel from the toolbox and set about to carve a face on the rock. He attempted to make a scary face, a monster face. Who knows why? When he finished chiseling the face on the rock, he returned to where he'd found it originally. He placed it on the downhill side of the large boulder in order for it to be seen by any and all who were heading back up the hillside from the cabin. When I first saw the creature's face Mike had created, it looked like a wolf to me. Perhaps because Mike's etching reminded me of the disc jockey in the movie *American Graffiti*, this new rock-face landmark was named Wolfman Jack.

Later that year, on a solo trip of my own, I was up at the cabin working on some things, primarily burning slash in the outdoor fireplace. The weather was perfect—mostly cloudy but no rain, with a slight breeze. During the day the temperature almost reached 50 degrees, but that night it got closer to 35 degrees and much windier. Because the window opening in the sleeping loft had yet to be enclosed, most of us would elect to sleep down on the bottom bunk closer to the warmth generated by the cast iron stove, where we would be out of any wind that would blow through the opening in the south gable. Regardless of the weather, I've always preferred sleeping in the loft.

Just before turning in and calling it a night, I stoked the fire exceptionally well, then climbed up into the loft, got comfortable in my sleeping bag, and started to drift off into a deep sleep. The cold breeze coming through the gable opening forced me to put on my stocking cap, but the added warmth caused me to fall asleep quickly.

In the middle of the night, I was startled awake by something breathing by my head. Some invader was climbing through the open gable window! In an instant, I had my flashlight turned on and pointing in the direction of some noisy, breathing animal. Somewhat panicked, I leaned back and away from this intruder who was instantly blinded by the light I shined in its face. The damn thing hissed at me and made a high-pitched, snarling sound. Afraid, I yelled as loud as I could in its face. I don't know which of us was more frightening or fierce in that moment, but apparently the opossum thought I was.

The ugly marsupial that had rudely invaded my private sleeping loft abruptly turned and climbed down the outside wall of the cabin; upon reaching the ground it looked back up at me and hissed again. Pissed, I immediately hopped down from the loft and grabbed one of the 12-inch round logs we used to sit on inside the cabin. I hauled it back up the loft ladder and carefully positioned it on the wide windowsill. Holding my flashlight in my free hand, I peered outside and looked down at this indignant, arrogant, and smelly opossum! Why do invaders all seem to have an entitlement mentality? My nocturnal nemesis looked up at me once again, seeming to complain that my flashlight shining in its face was annoying. Well, I was annoyed too, and decided that a 35-pound log landing on its disgusting face was the change of attitude it needed. I let the log fall to be certain the opossum wouldn't disturb me again, then retrieved two larger logs from near the woodstove and continued to practice my "carpet bombing skills."

⋏

Later in 1988, triangular plexiglass was added to the window opening in the southeast gable. Dave framed in and paneled the north-
east gable. The cabin was beginning to look very impressive. Gone
was the old 1800s look. Now there was a loft that could sleep two
adults comfortably. Mike would finish the porch deck that year. A
second window was eventually added looking out on the creek.

Rob labored long and hard during the summer months of 1988,
designing and building a natural-looking dam on the small, spring-
fed creek a few feet north of the cabin. During the time Rob and
Dave were initially building the cabin and during our major remodeling, all decisions on where and how to move rocks from the
streambed and surrounding area were carefully considered. Rob
made great efforts to ensure that the dam and pond looked like they
occurred naturally without any human intervention.

Dave's son Jacob was instrumental in helping Rob build the
dam. Together they rolled a 400-pound boulder to anchor the top
of the dam on the waterfall side. The pond side of the dam became
a very scenic place, perfect for getting drinking water. Soon it became a haven for frogs. Rob would eventually place rocks along
the outside edge of the pond, placing each stone perfectly in the
riparian zone. Now we had two ideal places to get a pitcher of
drinking water: from the pond or the waterfall side of the creek.
Rob mentioned to me once that it was physically difficult to stand
in the creek bed arranging and rearranging rocks with tennis shoes
on while the water temperature was 40 degrees. Insulated fishing
waders with some warm wool socks might've helped, but for whatever reason that never happened.

For over four decades, Rob, Mike, and Terry made many trips
to assess the cabin site after severe winter storms. Some years the
damage was light; others, it was extremely heavy.

As time passed, Mike and Rob decided to build a nice woodshed. One September they came up to the cabin and arrived at dusk
and chopped up downed (windblown) timber until it got dark.

The next day they started assembling the woodshed. Mike built the floor while Rob framed the roof and put up a couple rows of cedar shakes. They also removed the logs from the pond and sawed them into links, then split and stacked them to dry.

While heading back down the trail they cut up and removed twenty-five or thirty trees that had blown over the trail months earlier. Some were as large as eighteen inches in diameter. It should be noted that Mike wanted to leave all the trees that had blown over to slow down the number of visitors up the trail, but Rob thought it would be too hard to get back to the cabin with so many obstacles. A compromise occurred, so while they cut between eighty and ninety smaller trees, they did leave about six large trees that were between twenty-four and thirty-six inches in diameter lying across the trail to discourage "the tourists." It's amazing how much work Rob and Mike were able to get done. A few years later, a National Forest trail crew removed those large trees that were encumbering the trail.

🜪

Terry mostly helped Rob and me with maintenance and upkeep rather than building things. The porch was completely redone in May of 2013. That work crew included Terry, Rob, Mike, a couple of friends, and myself. In less than two days we removed the old porch boards, reinforced the foundation of the porch, and Terry cut and split new, 2-inch-thick cedar boards for the porch area. Everyone worked well together; we hoped the new porch would last at least fifty years. I know there have been others who have made contributions to the cabin's construction, repair, and remodeling. As time went by and others were brought to the cabin, many helped to maintain it.

✦

Time has marched on since the cabin was first built forty years ago. Things have changed. The original, cute-looking cabin with its low, flat, angled roof, was neither dark nor gloomy after our concerted remodeling effort. After our concerted remodeling effort, it was neither dark nor gloomy. The remodeled cabin had a steep, vaulted pitched roof that provided a very open feel. The two impressive Plexiglass skylights welcomed natural light inside, and the loft window provided a view of the natural beauty of the forest without ever having to leave the cabin.

Outside of the cabin on the front porch and just to the right of the door is an invitation, signed by *R*, to anyone who finds the cabin. The invitation is simple. "Welcome to Sally Lake Cabin. Please sign the guestbook inside and record your impressions." In the span of nearly forty years, at least 350 different people have visited the cabin. Most of the visitors are family or friends of Rob, Mike, Dave, Terry, or myself. Yet some are complete strangers to us. Many have recorded their impressions in the cabin journals.

It's fair to say that I used to have an issue with strangers coming to the cabin. Not that I had any right to prevent anyone from visiting the cabin, especially since it was built on National Forest land without a permit, which made it public property. I just didn't want to share this magical place with those I didn't know or trust. I certainly didn't want the authorities to be alerted and destroy the cabin.

The first "strangers" signed the guest book journal in July 1983. Many others used the cabin after that, especially after all the remodeling had been completed. So, it wasn't like I was unaware that strangers had found the cabin and were using it prior to 2011.

As was often the case, I was planning one of my visits to the cabin, and I checked with Rob to see if he wanted to join me. He was game, and the date and time were decided. Over the course of our conversation, Rob shared something that shook me deeply.

Rob had been talking with Mike, who mentioned that the father of one of his employees told his son that he had been hiking in the mountains and happened upon a very unique cabin. He said he stumbled upon it during the winter after following a mysterious set of tracks. The winter weather in the mountains can be crazy. It will rain, then freeze, then snow. Hikers stomp holes in the snow, which leave an easy trail for people to follow. People might wonder why a particular set of footsteps jump off the trail and decide to follow the tracks to see where they go, and that's exactly what happened in this case.

The description his father shared about this particular, remote cabin seemed similar to our cabin. Mike asked if any pictures were taken of their discovery. Sure enough there were, and those pictures were eventually emailed to Mike—the discovery of our cabin was confirmed.

When I saw those pictures, my first thought was that strangers were going to pin the location and post it all over the Internet. Everything was going to change. I worried that the next time I was there, some strangers would be there already because they would be able to find it through GPS. That thought really bothered me, because all the cabin principals had an unwritten code: We didn't use GPS to find the cabin—we used our natural senses to navigate there. Not even a compass. You had to be familiar with the area in order to find it.

I knew the day would eventually come when the cabin was no longer a secret, but I had been living in denial and wasn't prepared to deal with this new reality. For weeks I tossed and turned at night, imagining the worst. Keep in mind that for the past forty years I had only shared the cabin with family, a few friends, and Rob, Dave, Mike, and Terry.

I became possessive and protective about the cabin, and verbalized on a few occasions how unwelcome strangers would be were they to just "show up" at the cabin when I was there. Rob even interpreted one of my comments regarding strangers to imply that I would be hostile toward them. That is not true! In fact, I was at the cabin once with my good friend Kim. That afternoon we were sitting on the benches around the outdoor fireplace area, relaxing and enjoying the nice summer weather, when in the distance we heard some people talking and coming toward the cabin. I immediately tensed, wondering who was going to show up. Were they people I knew? I sure hoped so. Just before they crossed the cedar log bridge, I called out in a stern alpha voice, "Who goes there?!"

The reply came back in a friendly voice, "Sam."

As Sam and his hiking buddy reached the cabin porch, I introduced myself as John, one of the cabin "Principals." I asked Sam how he came to know about the cabin. He said his Aunt Lauren's husband, Mike, had brought him there once, and he was so impressed and had so completely enjoyed being at the cabin that he promised himself he would return. Sam's friendliness and connection to Mike, put me at ease. I welcomed him and his friend Brody and introduced them to Kim. Before long we were all sitting around the outdoor campfire area getting to know each other: four guys sharing stories and expressing our absolute passion for this part of the national forest, especially this special, pristine place.

Later we gathered around the warm, rustic campfire, having shared a great meal earlier that evening, and continued to talk further into the night. I haven't seen Sam since our initial encounter, yet that surprise visit taught me a valuable lesson about "strangers" and how they can become friends if we invite them into our world, even if it's only for a few hours.

Nearly eight years have passed since I received the email about two new strangers visiting and posting pictures of the cabin. Since then I've come to realize some very important truths about myself. Perhaps I'm not alone in the realization that we sometimes become unnecessarily guarded and even fearful of some people, especially strangers. The cabin was a magnetic place, but it created a paradox.

The declaration "Welcome to Sally Lake Cabin" implied that everyone who happened upon the cabin or knew exactly how to find it was not just welcome but invited to stay there, and I couldn't agree more. Everyone who visited the cabin was encouraged to write something in the journal sitting inside on the counter. Throughout those journals are hundreds of written entries left by many people regarding their experience staying at the cabin. Some are cryptic, others very brief, but several are very heartfelt and express their sincere sentiments as a testament to how they feel about the sanctuary that this cabin had been for so many of us.

Some visitors would return to the cabin and record their latest impressions about having come back again; in a strange way they became known as "distant friends" recognized only by their journal entries and an occasional gift left as a display of their appreciation and gratitude for their use of the cabin. Some asked to join us for our next work project and thereby contribute to the maintenance of the cabin. Some even left their phone numbers and contact information.

Personally, I struggled to decide which journal entries should be shared, knowing that some people's sincere feelings about their experience at the cabin should only be recorded in the cabin journals and not here. The entries that I've included touched me personally; they brought me a measure of joy and some made me laugh. I felt compelled to include some of my family members' reflections along with entries of those I know. They can be found in the "Notes" section at the end of the book.

One significant thing I came to realize is that "others" whom I did not know now may become future friends that I've yet to meet and would like to greet some day with outstretched arms of gratitude and appreciation. I think of them as friends because they were willing to make the difficult trek up the trail, pass by my favorite resting spots, and hike in either good or bad weather just to be able to pass by the Big Cedar Tree, cross the log bridge, and step onto the porch to be figuratively or literally welcomed by Rob, Dave, Mike, Terry, or me.

Chapter 9
Cabin Lore

"There's always room for a story that can transport people to another place." —*J.K. Rowling*

S ome real-life events should be remembered and passed on from one generation to the next, especially true stories that can transform individuals into legends. These stories can take you to a place you've never been, but somewhere real, where you imagine yourself doing something legendary.

Dave: The Human Mule

In November of 1986, Rob and Dave decided the cabin stove needed to be replaced. The existing Shepard stove wasn't great for cooking. Its primary purpose was to heat the cabin. The heat was hard to regulate and the stove had been damaged when bears invaded the cabin a few years back. On their way to replace the stove, Dave and Rob stopped by our house to use my backpack frame. They had determined that they were going to pack an entire cast iron stove up to the cabin. This new stove came from Rob's dad's workshop and was not very large, perhaps sixteen inches wide and twenty-four inches long, but probably weighed around 165 pounds. Dave was determined to carry the actual wood box up to the cabin. After we took the stove legs off and the baffles and bricks out, the cast iron wood box still weighed at least a hundred pounds, perhaps more. Rob took the lighter portion of the cast iron stove (sixty-five pounds or less): the legs, some stovepipe, and the inside bricks and baffles.

I like to think that I goaded Dave into carrying the cast iron stove up to the cabin. I would often challenge him to do extremely difficult tasks. He liked to push himself physically. Most people I know go hiking on trails at a leisurely pace and enjoy the scenery and the journey. Most of Dave's cabin journal entries reflected how he used running the trail as a part of his cross training for future running events. He prided himself on being able to reach the cabin from the trailhead in just over an hour. Keep in mind, one would be climbing almost 4,000 feet over the course of four and a half miles. Making the trek while carrying the cast iron wood stove would take many hours. That November day in 1986, Rob and Dave secured the stove to my pack frame then—drove to the trailhead.

In my mind I could see Dave when he first hoisted that beast of a pack onto his back. In that first moment when he settled the pack on his shoulders, he must have groaned. Undeterred, he moved forward. The weight on his back would cause him to hunch over a little more than normal. I know he would try to walk as upright as possible. Dave was a physical specimen to behold. His lean body mass was less than 10 percent. He could've easily posed for Michelangelo's sculpture of David. He was perfectly proportioned and ripped; Greek gods never looked that good.

The hike on the trail itself would be beautiful that fall day in November. The last of the autumn colors would be clinging to the trees, yet most of the leaves would be scattered along the trail for the first mile. On that first stretch there were bigleaf maple, ash, alder, and some oak trees along with a good number of Douglas fir trees. It had steadily rained a few days prior, so the trail would be wet and the smell of the leaves and needles on the ground would be a pleasant fragrance. This would be Dave's fiftieth trip up the trail to the cabin since 1979.

By the time Dave crossed the creek, which is only a half mile from the trailhead, his shoulders ached and his legs began to burn with fatigue. He had begun to slump over even more. Resting for a brief moment at the creek, he offloaded his pack and instantly felt relief from the heavy weight he had been carrying. The wood box was secure on the pack frame. Yet, without a way to secure the pack around his hips' sudden movements from side to side, the pack wanted to toss Dave around. His shoulders throbbed and began to chafe. Dave drank as much delicious water as possible. The next water source was much farther up the trail.

They finally reached the first significant viewpoint. The liquid refreshment the creek had provided back down the trail was an essential resource. Dave usually would jog up this half mile stretch easily. Not this day. As he slogged up this half-mile part of the trail, he might have been wondering how the Sherpas from Nepal could climb in the Himalayas well above 20,000 feet carrying just as heavy a pack, and do it with seeming ease. Dave clearly was not a Sherpa. He may have felt more like a yak. Resting became a frequent necessity, but while resting Dave refused to offload the pack that held the stove securely in place. His back, shoulders, and legs began to burn, and his breathing became more labored.

The next part of his journey was a steep climb through a small canyon. The trail has grades of greater than 7 percent, sometimes 10 percent. There are spots on the trail where 12 percent grades exist. In the spring and even up until the first hard freeze, there are always lots of shrubs, ferns, and other vegetation encroaching upon the trail. The stretch before the first switchback was such a place. Along the way there were two places with switchbacks that gave him some measure of relief. Back then, just as one reached the switchbacks, there were a few boulders that needed navigating. This was where Dave actually looked like a yak; his burden forced him to crawl on all fours in order to get past those rocks blocking the trail. Rob's pack was also heavy, and he needed to work hard to carry his load up the trail. Rob probably offered to switch loads with Dave, but I'm positive Dave would not even consider changing.

Dave stumbled and fell at a dangerous part of the trail. To avoid injuring himself from the weight of his pack, which surely would crush him, he turned just enough at the last second so the cast iron stove pounded the trail instead of him. In one quick instant Dave was looking skyward like a turtle that somehow found himself on his back. Injury avoided, Dave rested briefly and he and Rob laughed about the odd circumstance.

The next set of switchbacks enabled Dave to gather his strength until the trail turned and opened up into the canyon where he had to tackle the long, steep grade to the Lunch Tree. With his head down and more hunched over than before, Dave continued his journey. He needed the energy to refuel his aching legs and back. This time he would offload his heavy burden and rest for awhile and after some needed food, Rob helped Dave re-shoulder his pack. Quietly he groaned, knowing the next stretch of the trail was steep and included an area where boulders covered the trail again; requiring him to scramble over large rocks, once more on all fours.

Dave reached the cedar grove where a small spring allowed him to rehydrate. From the spring he needed to hike just 200 yards until he could rest again. The pain he was experiencing in his back, legs, and shoulders continued to haunt him. Having no other choice, Dave made friends with his pain. This was Dave's way to meet this difficult challenge.

Another long, steep part of the trail lay ahead. What pushed him forward and enabled him to cover this next part of the trail is what makes Dave truly unique. Fearless and resolute, he pressed forward. His burden was winning the battle, forcing him to take five to ten steps at a time, then rest and catch his breath. These steps were short strides, not the long strides he would make when running the trail. Now, more than ever, he must have felt like a human pack mule. More than another hour would pass before he would reach the last watering place along the trail.

Rob went ahead to offload his pack at the cabin, then returned to help Dave. As Dave reached the jump-off location, he was more motivated than ever to make it on his own. He just kept pressing forward, knowing that every step he took was a downhill step—except, of course, when he had to step over logs. Even when Rob came back to help, he continued to trudge onward. Rob wanted to take Dave's burden from him, but that would only happen if Dave collapsed. How Dave navigated down to the Big Cedar Tree without breaking his neck is beyond my comprehension. From the Wolfman Jack landmark to the Big Cedar Tree, one must carefully hike down a 60-degree slope (cliff of sorts) then follow a game trail, stepping over a few logs for about fifty yards to the Big Cedar Tree.

Dave found a reserve of energy he did not know existed. He covered the distance from the jump-off point and the Big Cedar within minutes. His friendship with pain would soon end. Dave reached deep within himself to muster his last bit of energy. Rob would not remove the burden from Dave's back. Stumbling to his knees many times over the last hundred yards, Dave finally reached the cedar log that led across the creek to the cabin porch. As he fell to the porch, his journey ended, and the legend of the Human Mule was born.

I've heard the story of Dave carrying the cast iron stove to the cabin dozens of times over the years. Rob has told me most of those versions, and somehow parts and pieces of this story get changed just a bit. No matter. Terry, his son Tom, and Rob carried the newer stove up the trail. It should be noted that the old stove was enshrined, so to speak. Its new home became part of the unique outside campfire cooking area. Rob did a marvelous job rebuilding the rock fireplace to include the original cast iron stove.

More than once I asked Dave about that monumental event. He was always very matter of fact and would downplay his accomplishment. You might have thought he was quoting the next to the last scene from the movie *Jeremiah Johnson*; when his mountain man friend and mentor, Bear Claw, asks him, "You've come far pilgrim, you've come far. Were it worth the trouble?" Jeremiah replies with an upward thrust of his chin, "What trouble?"

Dave did enjoy the fact that after that event, he was nicknamed the "Human Mule," a nickname that has stuck ever since. This quote from Alexandre Dumas is fitting for him: "Pain, anguish, and suffering in human life are always in proportion to the strength with which a man is endowed."

Terry and the Great Sniff

One winter, Terry and I hiked to the cabin a day apart from each other. I embarked before him; it was a heavy snow year, and I encountered snow well below the cedar grove. Carrying a heavy pack and my old-school snowshoes made it difficult to get through the grove of trees. It must have taken me well over an hour to get through that stretch.

Because I started hiking up the trail in the late afternoon, by the time I "turned the corner," it was dark. Fortunately I made it to the jump-off point. As I headed in what I thought was the best direction to the cabin, I was unable to locate the Big Cedar Tree, which is critical in navigating to the cabin without a compass. I knew I was less than half a mile from the cabin. Deciding it would make no sense to go any farther, I stopped for the night. A nearby Douglas fir tree donated some low hanging limbs, and those fir boughs made a comfortable bed to sleep on. I rolled out my tarp and put my sleeping bag in between the folded tarp, then began settling in for the night. My adventure with Rob in January 1971 taught me a lot about wilderness camping, especially in the winter.

The weather had changed, beginning to sleet and spit snow. The wind picked up, causing the surrounding trees to have that loud, familiar conversation as their limbs beat against each other. Whenever I'm out alone in the woods and sleeping outdoors, I always place my hatchet and flashlight right under my sleeping bag where they can be reached quickly, especially on nights like this one.

I had finally drifted off to sleep when suddenly near my head I heard something breathing or sniffing around my tarp. I tensed up, wanting to quietly grab my hatchet. Yet, I waited. The animal breathing near my head had me paralyzed. Was I going to be attacked? I lay there motionless, hoping the breathing would stop. The breathing sound faded, and I finally decided to confront my fears. In an instant, I grabbed my hatchet in one hand and flashlight in the other. I threw my tarp open determined to do battle with my enemy.

What? My bright light blinded no enemy eyes. No large, non-hibernating bear was sulking away or prepared to maul me. Neither wolf nor wolverine snarled. Nothing was out there, nothing, as I scanned 360 degrees with my flashlight. How in the hell could my enemy disappear so quickly? My heart rate had to be chattering around 180 beats per minute or higher. After several minutes of reexamining the area around me and seeing nothing but trees, I convinced myself I must have been drifting off to sleep and dreaming that I'd heard some predator breathing right next to my head. Finally, I pulled my tarp back over myself, got comfortable in my sleeping bag once again, slowed my breathing back to normal, and fell asleep.

The morning light beckoned me awake to several inches of fresh snow. I packed up my gear, surveyed my surroundings, got my bearings, and headed toward the cabin. It only took me fifteen minutes to get there. When I arrived, the cabin was empty and cold. There was ample dry wood, and I built a warm fire, changed into drier clothes, and started making some breakfast. I kept the stove filled with firewood, cleaned up, and read a few chapters from the book *Lonesome Dove*.

As evening approached, the weather got worse. A significant snowstorm was passing through. When I went out to fetch more dry firewood, six inches of new snow had already fallen. Terry didn't meet me at our agreed-upon meeting place, the jump-off point, and I wondered what time he would show up. Had we miscommunicated the day we both would start up the trail? I returned to the

Cabin in the Winter

cabin and made a nice dinner, thinking he would show up in time to share it with me. It was about 10 p.m. when, having long since eaten my dinner, I moved Terry's portion off to the side of the stove to be warmed up later. I went out onto the porch and crossed the creek via our cedar log bridge and pounded several times on a large cooking pot I'd brought with me. Listening to it echo through the woods, I kept thinking Terry would hear the sound and holler back. The snow was really coming down hard. In between pounding on that old cooking pot, I'd shout out into the darkness calling for him. I'd pause and listen, straining to hear his voice. No reply from Terry. I probably should've strapped on my crummy snowshoes and gone looking for him, but remembering the nightmarish night before, I instead wandered back into the cabin, put a few more logs inside the stove, got comfy warm inside my sleeping bag, and called it a night.

The next morning I warmed up the food that was set aside for Terry's dinner and scarfed it down. Then I proceeded to prepare for the hike back down. Once I reached the trail, I marched down the mountain as if I was being followed by a pack of wolves. Back home, I maintained for many years that it was a bear that put the fear in me that one night, mostly for the benefit of my children. Eventually I changed my story and claimed I was scared into almost cardiac arrest by a snowshoe rabbit. Bear stories are much more exciting than rabbit stories. At least I lived to tell this tale. And what of Terry? No miscommunication had taken place. He had had his own adventure to tell.

While I spent a cozy night inside the cabin, Terry was encountering his own set of difficulties on the trail. When he "turned the corner," it was dark and snowing like crazy. He had his headlight, but it was snowing so hard that the light reflected off the snow and he couldn't see ten feet. The snow and light were blinding. If he turned off his headlight, he saw nothing. If he turned it on, he saw nothing. He was in trouble.

At that point he figured, *John's not here at our meeting spot. . . .I suspect he's not coming. I'm out in the dark, I can't see diddly, so*

I'm just going to camp right here. He wasn't really prepared, but he wasn't unprepared. He was prepared for a bivouac, but he wasn't prepared to camp out. What he had was a big sheet of poly plastic and a sleeping bag.

Terry built a fire with some matches he brought, but of course he was on top of five or six feet of snow. The fire kept sinking down, because it was melting the snow, so it kept disappearing. He had a fire in the bottom of this hole, and continued feeding it wood while sitting about five feet above it. When you're out there, fire's your friend. Once the fire was going he was fine. He cooked up some stew and ate a sandwich, leaving a plastic bag with the stew can next to the campfire. Taking his plastic tarp, he draped it over a limb leaning against a tree. He crawled inside; it seemed almost like being in a mummy bag sitting in there with his feet in the bottom. He folded the plastic over the top of him, so he was pretty much enclosed.

The snow was still coming down heavily, but he thought, *I'm actually going to be able to sleep in this thing.* It was maybe only about 9 or 10 p.m., dark and peaceful and quiet. It had been maybe half an hour, and Terry was in a half-awake, half-asleep state. Then he started hearing thumps. He shot fully awake, and could hear sniffing outside. He thought to himself, *There is a bear outside this piece of four-mil plastic.* He took stock of his options. It wasn't going to be a good plan to go mano-a-mano with this bear, so he needed to scare the bear away. He mentally made a list of the resources at his disposal.

It was pitch black, and his best friend was probably going to be noise. He didn't have a gun or anything. What could he do for a bright light? Then he thought—*matches.* He dug out the book of matches and lit the whole book on fire. He threw it outside and screamed and yelled as loud as he could. He could hear the bear jump back and shuffle away—Terry's heart was racing, so he wasn't going to be able to go back to sleep right away. But he knew he'd dodged a bullet. It was dead quiet outside his plastic sleeping arrangements.

After about a half hour of wondering if the bear was gone. . .it came back. It was sniffing around, probably investigating the empty stew can Terry had left by his fire pit. He thought, *Oh man. My plan worked once, who knows if it will work again, but I don't really have any other options.* He planned to throw his light out there and leave it on. Instead, he started screaming and yelling, rattling the plastic tarp while shining the flashlight from inside his makeshift bivouac. The snow had stopped, so you could see the light pretty well, and luckily the bear jumped back again. Terry could hear it leave. It never came back.

Terry might have gotten an hour's worth of sleep. Just before dawn, since it wasn't snowing, Terry decided to gather up his stuff and head back down the trail. Looking around his primitive camp he saw bear tracks all around. The bear had chewed up the plastic bag with his remaining food and dragged it off somewhere. Terry was home in time for breakfast.

Rob's ChapStick

Rob has ventured up to the cabin hundreds of times, and occasionally found himself running out of daylight well before reaching the cabin. One March evening he was supposed to meet me at the cabin. I left earlier than Rob and arrived well before dark. Around 10 p.m., the thought crossed my mind I probably should go looking for Rob. I pushed that feeling aside, believing that he was probably going to be hollering the traditional, "What's on the spit?" greeting before too long, and the warmth of the cabin was like a magnet beckoning me to stay inside.

I filled the woodstove one last time before turning in, but I couldn't sleep. I lit the lantern and went out onto the porch, hoping to see Rob walking toward the light I held in the direction of the Big Cedar Tree. After standing there for a few minutes and hollering his name with no reply, I went back inside the cabin. I hung the lantern in its place, turned off its fuel supply, and by the time the light of the lantern faded into darkness I was inside my sleeping bag warm and comfortable.

Early the next morning, well before sunrise, I was startled awake by the sound of the cabin door being opened abruptly. Not completely awake and unsure who was barging in, I quickly grabbed my hatchet and sat up to look down on the miserable creature below me. The intruder was Rob, and as I look down upon him from my comfortable sleeping arrangements in the loft, he glanced up at me and mumbled, "Did I wake you from your beauty sleep? Are you nice and comfy, John? You could have at least kept the wood stove burning through the night!"

"Hey Rob, good morning. I expected you last night. What happened?" It was probably 6 a.m. Rob lit a lantern, and it illuminated him building his desired fire. Soon the cabin warmed up and became more welcoming as Rob began recounting his night spent in the woods.

⋀

Rob does not run around in the woods planning to be stranded with no equipment or supplies. He's not a bumbler, or careless when hiking. He knew on this particular trip there was really nothing for him to bring, except himself. I had brought all the food. There are extra sleeping bags at the cabin.

By the time he reached the spot to jump off the trail and head toward the cabin it was totally dark. He began bumping into trees, stumbling and falling. Trying to get to the cabin before dark he had run and walked briskly up the trail. The warmth he generated doing so was now gone, and he was getting colder by the minute. No more than 200 yards off the trail from the jump-off point, he was left with one reasonable option: stop where he was and make plans to hunker down. It was going to be a long night, and a very cold one. Sitting in the darkness he contemplated what to do next.

Taking an inventory of his surroundings and himself, he searched his lightweight jacket pockets and found an old paper-style matchbook with a few matches still inside—six, maybe eight. That was good news. He placed them back in his coat pocket to keep them dry and reached into one of his pants pockets and found the ChapStick he'd placed there just before he locked his truck and started up the trail.

Rob most often has a positive outlook and attitude regardless of the circumstances he faces. That night he would need to dig down and find his most optimistic inner self. Encouraged after taking inventory, he felt he had some of the resources necessary to build a fire. A thought came to mind: It would've been nice to have a pocketknife, and a flashlight or a headlamp. He promised himself he would carry some emergency preparedness hiking items with him on future treks in the woods.

It was dark. He couldn't even see his hand in front of his face. Sitting down he realized he could lean up against a fallen tree. Within arm's reach there were other standing trees, and on the ground around him were other fire-building materials. It was March, not July, and most everything he gathered up was a little damp. He needed some cedar or some tree bark with some pitch.

After several minutes of gathering and sorting through his fire combustibles, he handled every small stick and piece of bark with care, determined to know which and how much he would attempt to place around the first match he would strike. As he swiped the flimsy paper match across the tiny strip of abrasive sandpaper, he sheltered it from the wind. The match started to ignite, then abruptly dissolved into a minute smoke cloud.

Disappointed, he paused before his second attempt. As he struck the second match it produced a flame and he carefully added a small part of his ChapStick. As he imagined, the glob of petroleum jelly combusted, resulting in a much larger flame. He glanced down at his matchbook and saw there were about six matches left.

Carefully he placed the tiniest of twigs around his meager flame. He added a little more ChapStick to create more flame and heat. Suddenly the flame was gone. *Dammit, was there a slight breeze or were the twigs too damp?*

It was getting colder and Rob began to shiver from time to time, and he knew his core body temperature was dropping. Pushing that problem aside, he refocused his efforts on fire building. Inwardly he knew he had to get a fire going with the resources that were available, and he mentally told himself he was up to the challenge. Not willing to waste any more matches, he set out to find some cedar trees or a Douglas fir tree with sap oozing from its bark. Crawling on his hands and knees, he acted like a bear that was about to claw at every tree he came upon searching for honey.

Rob refused to crawl too far away from his starting point. Having been in the dark for perhaps two hours, his eyes had adjusted to the absence of almost all light, enabling him to partially see some objects a few feet away. Everything farther away than ten feet was totally dark and shapeless. After clawing on a few trees with no success, he came upon the remains of a tree stump that was the result of a forest fire that probably occurred a century ago. It was a cedar tree stump! Using his hands like bear claws, he ripped loose pieces of bark and dry wood chips. Once again, Providence had come to Rob's rescue.

Encouraged by his discovery, Rob gathered up several pieces of excellent fire-starting material and took them back to his fire-building area a few yards away. Huddling over, he created some shelter from the wind and changing weather. Wasting no time, Rob struck his third match and used several bits of petroleum jelly from his ChapStick, which ignited. Some of his newly found dried cedar kindling began to react to the heat. Delicately and cautiously, more tiny pieces of cedar were added to the fledgling fire. To his delight, the crackling sound of burning wood broke through the silence surrounding him. Little by little his fire became bigger, casting off light and warmth.

The temptation to build a bonfire almost overtook him. Using better judgment he decided on a nicely sized campfire, something he could keep contained in a forest full of windfallen trees and dead branches. His fire generated enough light that he could finally see into the forest for about thirty feet. The fallen log that he had been leaning against partially protected him from the weather.

Before cuddling up and lying alongside the tree, Rob set about gathering enough firewood to last through the night. Cold and hungry, he tried not to think about the dinner he was missing. *John always made sure there would be feast-like meals whenever he ventured up to the cabin. Did Sandy make some of her famous cowgirl cookies for John to take with him? If she did, would John fight off the temptation to eat them all before he showed up?*

Until breakfast, there would be at least eight hours of keeping the fire alive and trying to stay warm, especially if the weather got worse and began to snow or rain heavily. The night wore on ever so slowly. The wind picked up and the temperature continued to drop. What little moisture fell out of the clouds was some wet snow mixed with rain. Having no way to tell time, Rob simply kept his fire going and burrowed himself closer to his log shelter, trying to avoid getting wet when the weather acted up.

His shivering woke him; he had dozed off. Sleep was much needed, but his fire had been reduced to a few coals, almost extinguished. Regenerating the fire, Rob committed himself to stay awake in order to avoid being awakened later because his lifesaving fire had died out due to his neglect.

The side of his body that was up against the log was not really very warm. In fact, it was cold. The other side of his body facing the fire was toasty warm. He would build his fire until the heat was almost unbearable to lay next to, and then try to rest for bit, attempt to sleep (for perhaps fifteen minutes or so) until the cold side of his body became uncomfortably cold and craved more heat, then rotate and add fuel. One thing was for certain: His fire would never go out due to neglect. The pattern of tossing and turning then adding more firewood to the fire emerged.

As he began to re-stoke the fire for perhaps the twentieth time, Rob seemed to sense that dawn was not too far off and the twilight zone was emerging. The time between dawn and daylight is often the coldest. Rob lay in a fetal position up against his log companion, waiting for just enough light to travel. It was damn cold. He looked off in the direction of the cabin--he needed to be able to see far enough into the distance to make out trees and the contour of the ground at least a hundred feet ahead of him. Since his lifesaving fire had almost completely burned out, he stood up abruptly, stretching his stiff, aching body and readying himself to leave behind his nighttime ordeal in the mountains.

Just as he stretched one more time, he heard a loud screeching sound only a few feet from where he stood; it startled him so much that he jumped into fight-or-flight mode. He thought he was going to be attacked by a mountain lion that had just snarled at him, but before he could bolt from the danger, a second, louder shriek broke the silence. Bracing for an initial blow to follow the horrifying sound he'd just heard, Rob crouched to absorb the impact. Fear, total and complete fear, coursed through his veins instead of blood. One more bloodcurdling screech echoed through the trees. As he looked for where the sound came from, suddenly swooping down within a few feet of him was a very large…adult screeching owl.

That owl seemed to be telling Rob to get the hell out of his sleeping area. Rob gladly obliged—minutes later, he woke me up from my peaceful sleep in the loft of the cabin, grumbling about how the fire in the cabin stove had gone out.

⋏

Surprised

The cabin is on a small rise above a small lake, which we christened Sally Lake after the salamanders that live there. When you walk down the hillside from the cabin through some fairly dense forest, you'll reach an almost impenetrable spot near the shore where deciduous as well as evergreen trees grow in abundance. You literally have to break through the last fifteen or twenty feet of heavy foliage before popping out on the other side into the open-air, marshy area. Before you can reach the edge of the lake, you must walk across a boggy area for about fifteen or twenty feet. Just to the right of the bog, in the lake itself, is an area filled with lily pads.

One morning Terry wasn't trying to be stealthy, but he hadn't made much noise as he reached that spot. When he popped out of the trees and brush, he found himself standing about eight to ten feet from a big bull elk that was up to his belly in the lake, eating the lily pads. They both saw each other at the same moment. Both were startled, but the bull elk went totally crazy. He jumped up and down, thrashing back and forth, snorting like he was mad, and tried to get out of the water to run away. But of course, he was bogged down in the peat and marshy ground. The more he pushed and thrashed, the more he sank down into the muck, which only served to make him panic even more. The elk was literally churning the water like an eggbeater with his legs, trying to get himself out to escape. There was no way to help him calm down, so Terry just stood there and watched, feeling sorry for him. It took probably a full thirty seconds, which seemed like ten minutes, before the huge elk finally clawed his way to solid ground and took off through the woods, crashing through the forest like a freight train for at least a half mile, until the echoes of his escape finally faded into the distance.

⚱

The Valentine's Igloo

One Valentine's Day our daughters Emily and Desirae wanted to go on an adventure with me to the cabin. They had grown up hearing about several of my winter trips to the cabin and asked if we could hike there and do some snowshoeing. My answer was, absolutely! They suggested I invite Uncle Rob to join us. They loved being around Rob. He was always fun, interesting to talk to, and ready for an adventure. Rob readily agreed to meet us at the trailhead. We packed all of our necessary gear and drove from our small town in Idaho to Oregon. Arriving late that night, we stayed in a motel located about a thirty-minute drive to the trailhead.

Upon reaching the trailhead, the next part of our journey was pleasant, free of snow until we reached the Lunch Tree, where we ran into packed snow and ice. As Emily remembers, her deep green and light green dappled world of the mountain and forests had become an entirely new place. Nothing was very familiar to her, but hiking in the snow and the mountains was a majestic experience. Getting through the Cedar Grove was challenging. The snow was so deep there that we abandoned going on the actual trail and instead plotted a more direct course toward where we would "turn the corner."

After reaching the Cedar Grove, we stopped to rest. As we looked back from where we had just traveled, the view was stunning. The river, three miles and 3,000 feet of elevation below us, looked tiny in the distance. On the opposite side of the river more mountains vaulted upward, mostly covered in snow. They were partially shrouded in gray and white clouds. The scene I beheld was to be remembered forever: a stunning panorama that would make painters and photographers wish they could somehow capture on canvas or film what my eyes were seeing. Emily, Rob, and Desirae stood a few feet below me on the snowy mountainside with beaming smiles as they stood in the foreground of my majestic view. Seizing the moment, I became a photographer.

When we reached the cabin I was taken back by the snow depth—it was five feet deep or more. Rob's beautifully built oyster-shell-designed outdoor fire pit was completely buried. Walls of snow surrounded the porch, and navigating across the cedar log bridge was treacherous. The small stream, which flows less than ten feet from the cabin, was brimming with water. Making a small passageway onto the porch, we offloaded our packs. Rob set about making the cabin come to life as he built a fire in the stove. The girls waited patiently inside, sitting on the bottom bunk/sofa while Uncle Rob persuaded the wood stove to generate enough heat to turn the cabin from nature's version of a cryogenic chamber into a cozy den of warmth. After a rest, some food, and warming up, it was time to find something fun to do.

Nobody remembers who had the brilliant idea to build an igloo, but we build it we did. Rob, of course, engineered the build. Emily and Desirae were in charge of stamping down the snow as much as possible with their snowshoes, compacting it for Uncle Rob and me to cut out cubes. Emily really wanted to sleep in the igloo the first night and convinced me to join in the fun. We brought a lantern inside, relishing the hard snowy ground under our sleeping bags and the hollowness of the space. It was our fortress of solitude. This wilderness igloo was a memory Emily and Desirae could share knowing that in the 21st century, very few people have slept in an igloo they built themselves.

Mike the Quick Thinker

Mike made numerous trips to the cabin during the remodeling years. Most of those trips up the trail to the cabin meant his pack was heavy laden. When hiking, Mike typically hauled up supplies with Rob and often would encounter other hikers along the trail. Often, the big backpacks and odd cargo generated some very strange looks. Some hikers even asked where they were going and why they were carrying strangely shaped items up the trail.

Once, Mike was with Rob and they'd decided to take up a large garden rake and a big green container. Mike had the rake and Rob had the container. They were hiking up the trail and came upon two pretty young women. They all had to stop to get around each other, and one of the women asked what their stuff was for. *Why were they carrying that big green thing and a garden rake?* They hadn't rehearsed any sort of answer, and didn't know what to say. Mike ingeniously replied, "Oh, we're just hunting mushrooms." She looked at him with confusion, and he could see the wheels turning in her head. The two guys were going to gather mushrooms with the big rake and put them in the giant green thing? But she didn't question it, and they went on their merry way.

When Mike and Rob were hauling up the plexiglass for the porch, they both had 32" x 49" Lexan panels for the skylights tied onto their backs. They came across a guy who asked, "What the heck are you guys doing?" Mike, nervous, played it cool and said they were setting up some weather research experiment. Apparently the way he said it came out really well—his response mostly made sense, but was just confusing enough that the man didn't push further. Perplexed, the guy replied, "Oh, well of course. I understand. Carry on, boys. Have at it."

Mike's quick thinking meant these trail encounters were never embarrassing. However, one hot August day Mike hiked up with Dave when Dave was wearing his bikini underwear and nothing else. He and Dave headed up the trail as usual—but it quickly took a turn for the unusual. Dave, claiming it was too hot and he didn't want to get his clothes sweaty, stripped down to his bikini brief underwear. No shirt, no pants—just the underwear and a pair of tennis shoes. Mike tried to understand. It *was* a warm day…but, knowing Dave, he probably just wanted to show off. They came across multiple people on the hike up. Mike was embarrassed for himself and for Dave. Mike let Dave go ahead of him and held back. I can't blame him for that! Mike didn't recall anyone commenting to him about Dave (although a few people had odd facial expressions). He consciously stayed far enough back to disassociate himself from the strange sight of Dave hiking up the trail almost in the nude.

🜋

Brad's Attempted Airdrop

One year, Rob's brother Brad remembered how tough it was to hike the trail, so he had the self-proclaimed genius idea to fly over the cabin site and drop some supplies down. He had just received his pilot's license, and it seemed like an easy, cool way to stock the cabin without having to carry anything up the trail. He coordinated with Rob to make sure Rob would be at the cabin the day of the airdrop.

Swooping down over the forest on a bluebird day, he attempted to drop a box of supplies. He flew low and slow over the cabin site and pitched stuff out the window to hopefully land in the meadow on the edge of the lake. Not sure he had succeeded, he made one more pass and threw another box out the window. Rob was on the ground watching as Brad flew past, and he ran to the drop site and came across splattered cans and boxes completely destroyed.

Undeterred, Brad changed course and made another pass near the cabin to have some more fun. He launched a surprise attack, tossing a few dozen water balloons out the window. Neither effort proved particularly successful, with exploded cans of food scattered about and no water balloon hitting the spectators on the ground.

Chapter 10
Two Friends Lost

"One way to open your eyes is to ask yourself, what if I had never seen this before? What if I knew I would never see it again?"
—Rachel Carson

In 2017, shortly after I had returned from a bike trip, Mike called me. After a brief exchange of pleasantries, he asked if I'd heard from Rob. I told him no, I thought Rob was still vacationing in Australia. He thought so, too. He said Dave's daughter, Jennifer, texted him with news that Dave had died peacefully of natural causes at his home in Oregon. I was stunned to get that news.

When Rob returned from Australia in early November, he, like all of us, was still trying to deal with the shocking news that Dave had died. The celebration of Dave's life took place in November. I flew into town that Saturday morning and Mike picked me up at the airport. When I arrived with Mike and Lauren at the place of celebration, I immediately noticed there were well over 200 people mingling and waiting for the formal part of the celebration to start.

I immediately sought out Dave's son Jacob, and as we embraced I observed that he was just as stoic as his father would have been had their roles been reversed. Jacob had a big smile on his face and thanked me for coming. I gave him a manila envelope that contained some photos of his dad I thought he'd like as remembrances. There were copies for him and his sister Jennifer, who was greeting and thanking all the many people for coming.

Just before the formal part of Dave's life celebration started, Rob and I finally spoke for a brief moment. I could tell he was hurting inside and now that Dave was gone there was a huge void in his heart, and seemed to me that he wasn't exactly sure how he'd fill that space. I suspect Rob will fill that void with all the great memories he and Dave shared together. I know that's how I've filled my own void.

⁂

According to the Oregon Forest Resources Institute, Oregon wildfires charred more than 517,000 acres in 2017—nearly equaling the size of the state of Rhode Island—at a cost of $454 million. A representative with the U.S. Forest Service said in 2017 Oregon had 121 miles of national forest trails that were impacted. Some of the wildfires that year burned rapidly in dense timber; walls of fire swept through thousands of acres of forest, leaving over a million trees blackened and dead. It would seem to some as if this was something out of Dante's *Inferno*, nature's version of what the fires of Hell might look like. Many hiking trails were damaged and vast swaths of forest charred.

Terry was the first to make his way up to the cabin, taking pictures of the state of the trail and sharing his findings with us. That had been in late October. Now it was nearly December, and the Western Oregon high mountain winter snows were just beginning. Rob knew that because of the condition of the trails nearest the cabin, he would need to patiently wait until April in order to safely travel and see what Terry had told him.

When the day finally arrived, Rob decided to take a different route than the infamous trail we always took. This was due to the National Forest restrictions. This different route was the long way to get to the cabin, but his longer journey would be far less physically difficult (actually, it was mostly all flat) than the usual trail.

During the more than 6-hour hike, Rob occupied most of his mental time reflecting back over forty years of memories and amazing times spent at his wilderness abode. He could still see in his mind that singular day when he and Dave walked across the cedar bridge that nature created, crossing over a small stream that led to a tiny clearing, and then farther on, to the nearby small lake.

They were young stripling adventurers back then, fearless and undaunted. Rob had been eccentrically disposed to the notion that a cabin should be built in that small clearing; he had no idea back then how that decision would impact our lives and so many others.

For the first time in his forty-five years of hiking and bush-whacking in this area of the National Forest, Rob fetched his old 1970 Vintage Engineer compass from his pack to make sure he was traveling in the correct direction. Walking slower than normal, he noticed the usual vine maple, huckleberry, and wild rhododendron bushes were gone. Most of the trees were charred and dead. Those that survived were scarred and clinging to the earth around them.

Walking into this forest apocalypse was an emotionally wrenching experience. Glancing at his compass he thought he should be getting to where Wolfman Jack was usually perched. Should he keep heading due east? Where was the big boulder? Stopping to survey the surrounding area, he saw in the distance some large rocks surrounded by several dead trees. The fire damage made it easier to see through the woods. Walking toward those rocks he convinced himself that the big rock he was approaching was where Mike's Wolfman Jack called home. Yes, this was where Wolfman Jack had perched himself. Stopping briefly, he scanned the surrounding landscape and his eyes beheld a grove of forest untouched by the previous year's fiery blaze. It was just about a hundred yards down the hillside. Quickly, he made his way toward the stand of trees and saw the Big Cedar Tree, which had been spared its own personal inferno. His stoic Swedish and Danish ancestry would not allow him to shout for joy that the grand old Big Cedar Tree had survived. Instead, as a symbol of gratitude he gave his old sentential friend a rare embrace.

He marched quickly toward his only child, the cabin, and his emotions were beginning to consume him. As he placed his first step upon the cedar log bridge, he stopped himself, transfixed and temporally paralyzed. The very thing he had created, nurtured, molded, and transformed with the help of his cabin friends, was decimated.

⚜

Rob never had any biological children. Most of his eight siblings provided him the opportunity to become an uncle to many nieces and nephews. He became the "best uncle ever" to his siblings' broods, and even to our three daughters, Desirae, Meg, and Emily. During the summer of 1979, Rob's one and only child came into existence, and his devotion to this precious child became a most important responsibility. This cabin had become his life's legacy.

⚜

The cabin porch roof lay misshapen on the ground. There was no porch to step up on, no welcoming sign with Rob's infamous logo *R* to bid hello to any visitor. Nor was there any shelter to protect any and all visitors from harsh weather. The stainless steel that once framed a corner of the cabin was now toppled over and lay like a blanket covering the tin woodstove. The stovepipe was on the ground. The beautifully made cedar-planked floor that ran in perfectly designed directions was gone. The small wire mesh that was purposely sandwiched between those two layers of the cabin floor no longer deterred nor kept out small varmint-invaders. Instead, evidence existed that some pack rats were taking up residence. Clearly, there is a reason wood rats are so far down the food chain.

All the pots, pans, and cooking utensils were laying on the wire mesh covered in ash, mud, and tree needles. Most of the Douglas-fir trees that the cabin and its roof were framed and built around were severely charred. Perhaps because they were living trees at the time of the fire, they were mostly spared an inferno's death. By all indication, many will just stand as reminders of the hellish fire that passed this way.

Mike and Rob's woodshed had vanished. Even the latrine was destroyed. Its metal roof dangled precariously and easily could fall into the latrine itself if a perfect wind gust came along and untethered it from the few nails that held it in place.

The massive amount of devastation and destruction that surrounded Rob was taking its toll on his mind and heart. To combat that trauma, he quietly and reverently walked about the surrounding area reliving past happy memories created in this special place. His pain was the grief of death. Like the very fire that consumed his cabin, Rob was determined not to let the emotional sorrow and pain of the moment consume him.

A few hours had passed and twilight was full on, so Rob pitched the two-man backpacking tent he'd brought with him. There would be no fire tonight in his still-intact outdoor fireplace. What little food he'd brought with him he would save for tomorrow. It had been years since Rob had actually crawled into a tent up here. Before he dropped off to sleep, he found himself wishing he could relive his "screeching owl" experience just one more time, so he could find himself at the cabin again rousting me out of my peaceful sleep and grumbling about why I hadn't kept the stove fire going.

Morning came too early, and when Rob exited his tent he was determined to push back his feelings of loss and sadness. He built a small fire for some warmth, but mostly for psychological comfort.

The surrounding area became his personal archaeological dig. All the big metal items were collected and placed in a pile. The cooking pot, pans, and utensils had their spot. Rob found the old coffee pot still usable along with a few tin drinking cups. He set them on top of the old cast iron stove that Dave carried courageously up the trail so many years before. Rob was able to find every disfigured plexiglass window and skylight, and stacked them in their respective piles. The various tools, axes, hatchet, hammer, saws, and other sundry items like the hand drill wood rasp—even the extra nails—were gathered up and piled.

For several hours Rob scoured through the debris. He stopped occasionally to keep his comfort fire going and eat some of the self-rationed food he'd brought. He fought to keep his emotions in check. His mind worked feverishly to focus on his new mission, to gather all of the traces of human presence and devise a plan to make this area of the National Forest become where, "We Left No Trace."

Soon nightfall was beckoning, and instead of climbing into his tent Rob found a suitable log to sit on a few feet away from the fire pit. He heated up some hot water and wished he'd brought a few packets of Swiss Miss cocoa with him. Sipping on hot water would have to do. For the next couple hours he continued to mentally go over his plan, which was to remedy a problem that he never imagined he would need to resolve.

A spring rainstorm arrived during the middle of the night, making any restful sleep nearly impossible. As soon as it was daylight Rob packed up and left. When he arrived back to his vehicle he was totally drenched. Once he was within cell phone range, I received a call from him. I had known he was going to the cabin and was expecting a report, and I was not surprised to learn that he had a plan to make the cabin site as naturally pristine as when it was first discovered. Hearing Rob's perspective of what the fire had done grieved me and was painful to hear a second time. I had always thought the cabin would outlive all of us, and that a new generation would become its guardian and caretaker. Clearly, that was not to be.

Rob asked me to contact Terry and Mike, while he would call Brad and Dave's son Jacob. We all were to meet up at the cabin site in five days around noon and devote several days to Rob's plan. Everyone was to bring their own food, tents, rope for strapping things to the outside of their pack, and some extra-large and heavy-duty garbage bags. We were to also bring our own shovels. Rob would have Mike bring a garden pick-mattock. All were to bring our own pair of work gloves, and the need for several pairs of sheet metal cutting snips was discussed and agreed upon. We were told to plan on making several trips from the cabin site to haul loads of materials that needed to be removed.

Terry was the first person I called, and when I told him what Rob was asking of each of us, he said, "Absolutely! That's a great plan and I'm glad to be part of it. I consider Rob my friend, and right now he's hurting and has lost something very dear to him. I'll see you on Wednesday evening. Drive safe."

When Mike answered the phone, he was just as supportive as Terry. He said to me, "Robert just wants to make things the way they were when he and Dave settled on the spot to build the cabin. He knows damn well he can count on us to be there. I'll see you Thursday morning."

I arrived at Terry's house around 8 p.m that Wednesday and offloaded my pack into his truck. Terry and I picked up Mike at his house at 5 a.m. the next morning. We volunteered to take the usual trail to the cabin site to provide a report on how safe the trail would be. Rob, Brad, and Jacob took the long route to the cabin site so as to compare the routes and decide which one was best to pack out the several loads of debris.

Good weather was our friend while hiking, but the trail itself was a mess. My new hiking poles saved me several times from certain ankle or knee injuries. The first mile up the trail was unusually easy with no obstacles to traverse, but after that it was a bushwhacking adventure. The nearly five hours we spent hiking was almost entirely void of discussion about what we'd see once we arrived. Nobody wanted to talk about it. Instead, we commented how the forest fire had transformed the trail. There were several new land and rockslides we traversed, and large piles of charred dead trees crossed the trail. It was more than a mess; it was an obstacle course. Coming back down would be challenging.

When we approached the cedar bridge we ceased talking entirely. Crossing to the other side of the creek, the three of us stood side by side, spellbound at the sight before our eyes. Terry broke our silence, "This is much worse than I remembered." We each wandered about the area attempting to take in what we were seeing. Our silence continued. What Rob and Terry each separately described had now become a reality for me. Rob and his group had yet to arrive. I went and set up my tent away from the planned work area. I grabbed one of my PB&J sandwiches and walked down to the lake. When I returned to the cabin site, Terry and Mike were building a small fire in the outdoor fireplace. They pitched their tents not far from mine.

All of us wandered around in silence for several minutes. After what seemed like about ten minutes of contemplation, I broke the silence, quietly exclaiming, "Never in my mind could I have imagined or create a scene like this." I held back speaking aloud my next thought of, *I guess the wilderness pentathlon days are over?* This was not a time for insensitive humor. I sure hoped the next few days would not be this somber.

Rob arrived with Brad and Jacob, and he gave them some time to process the scene they beheld before gathering us all together to discuss his plan. The area where all of our tents stood looked like a cleaned-up version of a homeless area one might see under the Steel Bridge in downtown Portland, Oregon.

As we stood around the campfire, Rob explained his plan to remove all the cabin materials. To my surprise he had changed his mind about hiking here via the longer route and instead his group had hiked the traditional trail, too, just a couple hours later than we had.

We would each haul a load of material down tonight, arriving around dark, and return as a group with our empty packs, hopefully before midnight. He said we'd do the same thing tomorrow and Saturday, if necessary. I thought to myself, *I've never, in all the years hiking the trail, hiked up and then back down, to return again in the same day—let alone three days in a row. I'm nearly sixty-seven years old, not twenty-seven.* I wondered how the guys were convincing themselves that they could physically do this. Jacob was in his early forties and looked very fit. He was almost a clone of his father, Dave, so I imagined he wouldn't have very many feelings of self-doubt about the task at hand.

Before the first caravan of cabin rubbish removal departed, Rob required all of us to bring our headlamps, some food, and fill up our individual water bottles. We arrived at our trucks about 8:30 p.m. We stayed together as a group in case anyone got injured or needed help. I felt like I'd jogged down the entire trail. Luckily no injuries, but my quads were screaming out in pain. We quickly emptied our cargo into Terry's truck and started back the same way we'd just come. My sore shoulders, which had been carrying over fifty pounds of weight for the last four miles, were relieved to have no real weight to carry back up the trail. My legs ached, but I kept telling myself, *Just make friends with this pain.*

We made only one brief stop at the Lunch Tree. I needed food that would give me some energy, and I knew everyone else did, too. I offloaded my pack, opened up the top pocket, and retrieved a zip lock bag, announcing, "Gentlemen, I have a couple of Sandy's cowgirl cookies for each of you."

For a brief second the news didn't register in their minds, then Rob exclaimed, "We love you, Sandy!" and took his share of cookies. The others did the same and voiced their appreciation. As we pressed forward again I began lagging behind the others and became somewhat hypnotized by the five headlamps lighting the trail ahead of me. They were like shining beacons guiding me all the way to the cabin site.

We stumbled into camp at around 11:45 p.m. Just before we arrived it had just started to rain, and everyone immediately went to their respective tents. I don't remember when the rain stopped that night. What I do remember was being awakened by Terry shaking my tent, saying, "John, wake up. Get up and come see this."

I said, "Seriously Terry, give me a minute." When I finally crawled out of my tent I felt more like a petrified human cricket. I could barely move. Terry was waiting over by the campfire, which he'd just revived from its night of slumber. "Okay Terry, what did you want me to see? It better be important."

He said, "Follow me, and be quiet." We stealthily walked down to the lake and before we broke through the few remaining places where bushes thrived, Terry softly said, "Be very quiet as we walk out to the edge of the lake." There, twenty feet away, was Rob. He was laying on top his camping tarp inside his sleeping bag.

"Why did he move out here by the edge of the lake?"

Terry whispered back, "I'm clueless. Perhaps he wanted some solitude."

We were just about to turn around and head back to the warmth of the campfire for some hot chocolate when the sound of Rob's voice broke the silence of the moment and he asked, "What's on the spit?"

I replied, "Grown particular?"

His reply surprised me. "Not today, not today."

I responded, "Come on Rob, come join us for some hot chocolate and our fancy potluck breakfast." The cinnamon raisin bagels I had saved for today were a hit with everyone. We all consumed the entire dozen as the sun was rising. Some in the crowd probably wished they'd brought some instant coffee, but hot cocoa would have to do.

Brad and I comprised the crew that was going to take the sheet metal cutters and reduce the metal from the various roofs to small-enough pieces to be stuffed into six different backpacks. That took three hours, mostly because of how the metal had been misshapen from the fire. Plus, it was very difficult to cut through the double-lined stovepipe.

In the meantime, Rob and Mike began carefully scouring through the cabin archeological site for all the glass from the broken windows, whiskey bottles, and every other evidence of human artifacts they could unearth. Terry was tasked with cutting up the former plexiglass windows to transportable sizes.

Mike had been working with Rob for several hours where the cabin once stood, and I overheard him say to Rob, "I found Wolfman Jack, and the re-etching of his face I did several months before the forest fire is still intact. I left it propped up against the cabin wall next to the cedar kindling pile; it must have fell face-down when the fire was burning the cabin."

Rob replied, "That's amazing." I looked up to listen more intently to their non-private conversation when I saw Mike stand up and begin walking by the area where I was working with two objects in his hands: the hand-crafted door-bolting mechanism he'd designed for the cabin door and his friend, Mr. Wolfman. He headed directly toward his tent and placed his keepsakes inside his tent door before walking back to work with Rob. As he walked past me I caught his attention and asked, "How are you doing Mike?"

He had his trademark grin on his face and replied in typical Mike fashion, "I'm fine, John."

Around noon we all stopped working and made a potluck of our respective lunches. The lunch conversation consisted of some voices of gratitude for how the cabin brought each of us closer as friends and family. We did not talk of the cabin any longer. What we did discuss was how it would be necessary to make another down-and-back trip, just like the day before. No one whined or moaned about the pending difficulty of the task ahead. Mike actually made us all laugh when he asked, "Alright John, what treats do you have to share with us later tonight when we pass by the Lunch Tree?"

I replied, "You just wait and see, I promise it will be worth the journey."

I fell twice on my trip down the trail. Nothing serious happened to me, but my legs were aching and feeble. It seemed like they could buckle beneath me at any time if I wasn't more careful. Being the last hiker in our group, I watched the others to see if they, too, were struggling. They all looked to be doing okay.

Terry was taking the lead and babbling about something to Jacob. I couldn't hear their conversation. Rob, Mike, and Brad were moving cautiously down the trail in front of me. Neither Mike nor

Rob was talking. Brad, on the other hand, had been telling one of his many amazing work-related stories. Keep in mind, Brad is a private jet pilot, and he was sharing a story about one of his recent trips flying a medical team from Anchorage, Alaska, to Seattle, Washington. Their cargo was a human heart that had been removed from a young man who died in an auto accident. All the details, descriptions, and demands that Brad shared about that trip painted a picture in my mind that occupied my thoughts until we arrived at our trucks for the second time in two days.

We each unloaded our packs of cabin artifacts in the back of Rob's SUV. All of us looked spent and no one seemed to be in any hurry to begin the trek back where we'd just come. I checked my watch and it was almost 8 p.m. Hunger was getting the best of me, and we all knew there was a small burger joint about ten miles away. If we wanted to, we could drive there in about fifteen minutes to retrieve a much-needed meal. The question was, who would make that suggestion? I decided it was my duty to pose the question and see if everyone would agree. It had to be a unanimous consent. "Hey, what do you say we jump in our rigs and go to Ed's Drive Thru to get a burger before we head back up the trail? If we call ahead now to order our food, it could be ready by time we get there." Rob was the first to agree to the plan, and everyone else jumped on board. The phone order was placed and we arrived with perfect timing. The hamburgers and fries had just finished cooking and we only had to wait a few minutes for those who ordered milkshakes. On the way back to the trailhead I actually paced myself and ate slowly, fearing if I ate too fast, I might have issues while hiking back up the trail. That would be the last thing I needed.

When we arrived at the Lunch Tree to rest briefly, I asked if everyone wanted the snack I'd promised. To my surprise, they all said their dinner was food enough for the night. I said, "Okay, I'll share my treat with you guys tomorrow." The delicious dinner provided all of us with much-needed energy. With some of my strength restored, I was able to keep up with my cabin friends as we all trudged back to our little tent city in the wilderness.

We all seemed aware that our last day here didn't require an early start, but the morning blue skies rousted us awake and inspired us to get going. The last of the Swiss Miss cocoa packets were shared, and I busted out the treat I'd promised the day before. My raspberry oatmeal bars were a hit.

The fire in the outdoor fire pit was extinguished. Most of us had our packs filled and were ready to head back. Rob's plan was nearly completed. We all stood there looking around, anxious to get back to our respective homes. The last remains of the cabin were Rob's oyster-shell-shaped fireplace and the old cast iron stove that Dave had hauled up so many years ago.

We were all within five feet of each other when Jacob's deep voice broke the silence of the moment, and it trembled when he said, "I really wish Dad were here with us. We could have really used his help." Stunned, we all softly concurred with him, not knowing if he was going to say anything more, and perhaps a little nervously wondering what he would say next. Then, he said, "Uncle Rob, will you help me secure the old cast iron stove to my pack and I'll carry it down the trail? It only seems fitting to me that I should do that to honor my dad."

My head was bowed when I heard Jacob ask Rob for his help and I instantly looked up to see the faces of my dear friends. Everyone, including me, was brushing away tears of joy from our faces. Rob looked directly at Jacob, nodded his approval, and said with a voice of astonishment and respect, "Sure, Jacob, I'd be honored to do that for you."

Everyone looked ready to hoist their packs on their shoulders and head out when Rob said, "Why don't we all take several armfuls of the fireplace rocks and place them along the river bank where they came from? It shouldn't take long." He then supervised our rock-carrying trips, making sure all the rocks found a natural place to reside up and down the creek where they'd originally once lived.

Rob and I helped Jacob get his pack situated on his shoulders and ready for the journey. The climb from the Big Cedar Tree to

The Cabin

Wolfman Jack's last-known residence is somewhat like freehand rock climbing up a 100-foot hillside, and Jacob's new burden would test both his mental and physical strength very early in his own "Human Mule" journey.

Nobody helped Jacob carry his pack there or anywhere down the trail. As Jacob clawed his way up the hill he groaned under the weight of his burden. The sounds he made were a verbal explosion of noises that some athletes make when they reach for the last bit of strength to do just one last repetition in their weight-lifting routine. All of us watched in awe as we saw Jacob conquer that hillside.

When he did fall because he got off balance due to the steepness of the trail, Jacob would find a way to get back up, miraculously uninjured. Just like his father had done many years ago, Jacob never moaned, complained, or offloaded his pack until he reached his destination. Somehow Jacob got through his journey; was it because Dave was walking right next to him the entire way? I believed Dave was walking with Jacob, perhaps even carrying his burden for him when it was needed most.

🔺

He was a young man of proper wit and an adventurous spirit, suited to the mountains.[1] Rob wanted to build a small, Jeremiah Johnson-like cabin, somewhere deep into mountains where he roamed. Searching, wandering, and exploring would eventually lead to the discovery of a small lake and one unique fallen cedar tree that crossed a small stream, which was not far from a very Big Cedar Tree. The cabin he built with the help of friends would over time become one with its natural surroundings. Jeremiah Johnson would have been proud; Rob certainly was.

On this last adventure, we came together again as friends like we've done so many times over the years. We were resolute, unwavering, undaunted, and determined to help Rob resolve a crisis, to make restitution, and we did. We left behind no trace, and now we just have our memories. What are those? They are the friendships we've made over the past forty years, not just at the cabin but elsewhere. The cabin is gone and as tragic as that may seem, my unwavering belief is that our relationships are far more important than the cabin or the forest where it once lived.

Our past shared experiences still live, not by the Big Cedar Tree that leads to where the cabin once was, but within this story and future stories worthy of telling. True friends are the essence of human relationships; the very reason to live, to love, they bring us lasting happiness and joy.

Epilogue

M y friendship with Dave spanned nearly fifty years, and I have many fond memories of the times we shared. As younger men, we (Dave, myself, and Rob) would get up early in the morning to ski to our hearts' content on the Willamette River. We would challenge each other to ski harder, do strange water ski tricks, and see who could produce the largest spray while making a beautiful slalom turn.

Once after Dave ran a half marathon in Eastern Oregon, he, Rob, and another friend competed in a rodeo: "The Wild Horse Race," in Spray, Oregon. They took second place. Dave claimed they would have placed first had Rob not taken so long removing the saddle from the horse. Of course, our shared cabin adventures are priceless memories, never to be forgotten.

Dave easily could have lived comfortably in many different centuries or time periods of human civilization. If he had access to time travel, I could actually see him joining up with Roald Amundsen as a crew member on The Gjoa, the ship Amundsen used to sail through and open the Northwest Passage between the Atlantic and the Pacific. Amundsen and his crew arrived in Nome, Alaska, on August 30, 1906. Instead, in more contemporary times Dave traveled to the northern latitudes of Norway so he could get as close as he could to the artic circle and glimpse the Aurora Borealis. Perhaps he even visited Amundsen's hometown.

I know that he traveled to Europe, Africa, and some parts of Asia. I'm not sure if he ever traveled to the Himalayan Mountains, but I know he was convinced that mountaineer George Mallory was the first to summit Mt. Everest in 1924. I can see Dave going back in time and joining Mallory and his climbing companion Andrew Irvine. Why would Dave do such a thing? Because if he could have, he would have!

If you were with Dave camping and sitting around a nice campfire, he might wax almost poetically about his trilogy of ancient Greek philosopher friends: Aristotle, Plato, and Socrates. I couldn't tell you whom he admired most, nor does it matter. I can clearly imagine Dave sitting in a room with each of them discussing a theory or idea and having a wonderful debate on the merits of time, the universe, and human nature.

Dave was my friend. He was Rob's best friend. He meant a lot to many people. He was a deep thinker and he lived his life on his own terms. Whatever life's challenges came Dave's way, he never let them define him. He is an icon. A picture of him was hung on the inside wall of the cabin, above the window that looked out over the creek. Rob rightfully framed his picture because Dave was one of the original cabin builders, and that specific picture evokes an image of a person who was building a cabin using hand tools. That picture looks like it could have been taken in 1829 instead of 1979.

We last spoke in June 2017, and we agreed that I would visit him later in the summer so he could tell his account of The Human Mule story once again. He seemed pleased that I wanted to write about him as it related to his involvement in the cabin. I regret we did not get the chance to have that conversation. I will be forever thankful to have known Dave and I will never forget him nor the positive impact and contribution he has made in my life. Since Dave passed away, I suppose some of us have thought about how much longer we have left on this earth. I know I have.

Rob retired a few years ago. Most of his adult life he worked as a software engineer, and and he spent most of his non-working life on adventures. He floated several hundred miles of the Yukon River in a canoe with Mike. He's traveled in many parts of Europe and the Middle East. He spent several months working on a unique engineering project in Kuwait. Often he can be found in the mountains of Oregon before and during elk season, tracking down elk just to capture pictures of them. To list all his non-cabin adventures, even just the ones I've shared with him, would require another book.

Road cycling is one of his many passions. He married a remarkable woman from Down Under, June, and they travel often. They love snow skiing and being out in nature making new adventures together.

Rob has been an extraordinary uncle to all of his nieces and nephews. Our daughters, Desirae, Meg, and Emily grew up calling Rob their uncle. He is a very giving person, not only of his time but his resources. Sandy and I would be remiss if we didn't acknowledge his acts of generosity toward us. Rob can frequently be found doing various projects around his mother's house. Jean turned ninety in 2018. When Rob's not traveling on some adventure, the Greater Portland, Oregon, area is his home base.

🦅

Terry divides his life up into three areas: working hard, playing hard, and doing nice things for other people. If you're going to keep up with Terry, you're going to have to have a lot of high energy and not be afraid of getting up early and doing a lot of things over the course of a day. I went deep-sea fishing with him a few times, and I was never so exhausted in my entire life. Up at 4:30 in the morning, take the boat down to the bay, launch it, put out crab pots, go fishing fifty miles out in the ocean for tuna, come back, fish for bottom fish, harvest the crab pots, and head back into the tiny bay before dark. Then we'd spend two hours cleaning fish. He loves fishing. He's positive and fun to be around.

Like Rob, Terry has traveled extensively in Europe, China, Southeast Asia, the Middle East, parts of Africa, and South America. Antarctica is probably on his bucket list. A few years ago, he and his wife Laraine spent three years in Singapore, where they served a church mission. They have three adult children and nine grandchildren who they often spend time with. They've lived in a small town in the Willamette valley of Oregon for the past thirty years.

Mike has owned the family business for nearly forty years and he still actively runs it, which directly impacts the lives of many people. He could be retired, but he isn't. When he is not working, he might be found making his own amazing rock outdoor fireplace on his property in Central Oregon. He enjoys fly-fishing with his younger brother Terry, especially on the Deschutes River in Oregon. He is married to Lauren, and they split most of their free time between their home in the Portland area and their place in Central Oregon. Like Rob and Terry, Mike has gone on many non-cabin adventures with Lauren and other friends, including summiting several mountain peaks in the Oregon Cascades. He and Lauren have traveled to many places in Canada and the United States. In October of 2016, Sandy and I went on a trip with them to Yellowstone National Park. We spent four days there, doing a lot of hiking and reliving some of our previous hiking glory days.

As for me, Sandy says I'm "Pre-tired." Over the past thirty-five years, Sandy and I have regularly gone on hiking adventures together in parts of Idaho, Montana, Oregon, Utah, Washington, Canada, and most recently England.

For the past fifteen years, road cycling has become a passion of mine. Rob and I have completed several "ride your age" trips in Oregon and Idaho. We did a 100-mile cycling adventure in the Palouse area of Northern Idaho. Terry, Rob, and I rode in two separate 100k cycling events, one in 2016, the other in June 2017. My regular cycling friends here in Idaho are awesome, and they have included me on some epic rides including the LOTOJA (Logan, Utah to Jackson Hole, Wyoming) and the Four Summits near Cascade, Idaho.

I never imagined I would ever write or even publish any book on any subject. Writing *By the Big Cedar Tree* has been a wonderful adventure for me and has resulted in my realization that everyone has their own story to tell about events in their lives and things that they have done and overcome, all of which have helped them face their own life challenges fearlessly with faith and gratitude.

Notes

In this section of the book I have included a detailed list of notes, references, and citations for each chapter in the book, even the Epigraph and Introduction. Hopefully most readers will find this list to be sufficient.

I fully expect that I have made a mistake somewhere in this book—either in not giving credit to someone where it is due or in attributing an idea or event to the wrong person. I apologize in advance.

Epigraph

In one of the last cabin journals, I read an entry signed by JQ, someone I do not know and someone I believe has been to the cabin several times over the past ten years. His journal entry on October 25, 2015 was eloquent and profound. To me it captures similar feelings I have had when I was about to leave the cabin and head back down the trail to civilization. For that reason, I used almost his entire journal entry as the Epigraph. JQ, you are truly a respectful friend of the cabin.

Introduction

The reference of "cabin principal" is used to denote individuals I consider to have been "principally" and actively involved in the cabin for decades. Rob was the cabin principal builder in 1979. Dave and Rob's brother helped him in that effort. I was with Rob when we found the general location of the future cabin site in 1974, not far from where it was actually built. Mike and I became involved in the cabin remodeling shortly after the second wilderness pentathlon event, and have been principally involved ever sense. Terry became principally involved in the cabin through his participation in regular general maintenance and planned cabin projects from 1988–2017, a span of twenty-nine years. A few years ago, Rob took a sabbatical from his role as the cabin overseer, and asked Terry to take that role. Terry accepted. Thus, the term "cabin principal" is used to represent myself, Mike, Terry, Dave, and Rob.

Chapter 2

1. https://en.wikipedia.org/wiki/Columbus_Day_Storm_of_1962
2. https://en.wikipedia.org/wiki/Great_Gale_of_1880
3. https://www.oregon.gov/ODF/Documents/ForestBenefits/WesternRedCedar.pdf

Chapter 3

4. https://en.wikipedia.org/wiki/Space_blanket

Chapter 5

5. https://en.wikipedia.org/wiki/Froe: A froe (or frow), shake axe or paling knife is a tool for cleaving wood by splitting it along the grain. It is a shaped tool, used by hammering one edge of its blade into the end of a piece of wood in the direction of the grain, then twisting the blade in the wood by rotating the haft (handle).

6. A misery whip is a two-man crosscut-logging saw, usually about seven to eight feet in length with handles. These large two-man crosscut saws were called "misery whips" because they were miserable to work with. They were used in logging to cut huge trees like the Douglas fir, redwood, and cedar trees in Northern California and the Pacific Northwest. They were also referred to as "whip saws." They have oak handles that can be easily removed with a turn screw if they break during use.

7. https://www.theatlantic.com/photo/2015/05/the-eruption-of-mount-st-helens-in-1980/393557/

8. https://www.forbes.com/sites/robinandrews/2017/01/08/this-is-how-a-volcanos-pyroclastic-flow-will-kill-you/#16c9e24932cd

Chapter 6
9. Quote from the movie *Jeremiah Johnson*, 1972

Chapter 7
10. Cabin Journal, Guest Book #2, Sunday, August 31, 1986

Chapter 8
11. Rodents of Unusual Size: https://princessbride.fandom.com/wiki/R.O.U.S.

I have included several notable cabin journal entries below for remembrance.

My first impression of hiking to the cabin must have been when I was really young. Too small to carry a backpack, and I distinctly remember everyone being much, much taller than me. I have the impression of dappled light shining through the trees, and just this feeling of being in a green lush world that was so large and far from anything. I felt distant from the world as I knew it, and that impression would return each time we would go back. But I remember that feeling of feeling like we were alone in this green world.

And the salamanders! I remember trying to catch them by the cabin and watching them scurry around Sally Lake. I can still recall their tiny, uber fragile little bodies, that aren't slimy. I had never held a living thing as delicate as those salamanders.

There's a spot on the trail where you veer off into the wild, and I remember this spot with anticipation. I always told myself that I would recognize it when we got there, but the trail to the cabin frequently was so grown over that I had to trust my dad to get us to the right spot. This point in the hike is probably my favorite. There's this feeling you get when you leave the established trail....one of freedom, and stealthy-ness. I truly can't describe the feeling, but its something I wish everyone could experience. This independence and escape and wildness about walking through the ferns and over moss covered fallen tree trunks until you get to the Big Cedar Tree, which then leads toward the cabin. While hiking I felt like a character in a story, a heroine trekking through the wild forests; just add flowers in my hair and a little more sunshine (it really did rain a lot). The reality is a little less romantic, with hair tied up in a kerchief or in a hat, layers of clothes and a plastic poncho to ward off the morning dew that covered.... everything. And then when the outdoor fire has been built the smell of burning cedar and Douglas fir wood will also mean that the food will taste fantastic...because my Pops hauled up all kinds of heavy and impractical things to eat. Someone brought up a watermelon once. I think Uncle Mike or Rob; someone also ran up ice cream. (And yes, to this day, the concept of RUNNING up to the cabin for the afternoon seems insane), but "my uncles" (Rob and Dave) did so. But the taste that I associate with the trips to the cabin has to be...of course...my mom's cowgirl cookies.

Going to the cabin was a social event. Countless stories told over and over, and playing cards or chess, or sitting by the fire reading a book (me). It was in a time before cell phones/iPads, so not having those things was normal, but today it's almost a foreign idea. And that was the point. Some days we didn't do anything but just exist in a wild space far away from everything you normally couldn't get away from. But other times we would go to the lookout point (if you wanted to hike more, ha!) and stare at the view. It's those moments of appreciating nature that some people have never experienced, and it's why I wish everyone had a cabin to visit growing up like I did.

Emily

✦

The cabin has been a major player in the years of our marriage, in a good way. Just the knowledge that John has had a place to go and get away from stress and the craziness that life can be, has been a positive for us. A blessing you might say. In the scriptures we read that when prophets wanted to talk to God, they went up the mountain. I never discouraged John from making the trip. It was good for the mind, good for the heart, and good for the soul!

I love all the memories I have of the small, rustic, unbelievable cabin in the beautiful lush terrain of Oregon. I can't even imagine our lives without it. It is part of our history, part of our lives forever. How grateful I am that those guys, so long ago, who took their quest for adventure in a positive, meaningful direction and built something that has created a joyful legacy for so many.

Sandy

✦

"The Cabin" and the many stories surrounding it were the fairy tales of my childhood. I remember as a very young girl hiking the trail, eating cold waffles out of snack bags and trying to be tough and walk as far as I could without help.

As I grew older I was so proud to declare to all my boyfriends and some of my high school classmates the fables and facts about my dad who was a "rebel and outlaw"; who with my uncles built (in my mind) the coolest cabin in the national forest, without using modern tools. Being one of the lucky ones who had seen it with my own eyes, I had become part of the legend in each trip I made into the forest.

I never grow tired of hearing my dad or Uncle Rob reminisce about those first adventures, (and I am eager) to add my later childhood experiences to their memories.

If only I could have been there from the beginning...I think, this is the appeal of the cabin for me; the allure of leaving the craziness of a modern world behind, enjoying the bonds of friendship, and building a haven with your own hands.

Meg

🌲

I met John in the spring of 2002. I got to know John as more than just a father of several daughters, but as a really great guy. He had some great stories. One I remembered most vividly was about "The Cabin." I kept hearing about this rustic cabin built way back in the forests of Oregon. I was working in Eastern Idaho one summer, and John and Sandy invited me to the cabin! THE CABIN!

The trail started under the canopy of massive cedars and Douglas firs. Everything was covered in moss. It is definitely like a rainforest, but lucky for me it was sunny that day! We hiked for three to four hours that day. We stopped at the lunch tree, a tree hollowed out by rot and a little help from Rob. We made it past the switchbacks past lookout point. We continued through the cedar grove when we reached the cutoff point. John then started going off trail down a steep hill! I continued to follow. He seemed to be following invisible clues because I would have certainly been lost at that point.

He finally said, "We're here." I said. . .where? "The cabin" John replied. I looked around and saw nothing. Then. . .it ap-peared. Similar to those 3D images you'd have to look at on paper for a long time before you could see the images. The cabin just appeared. Even though I was looking at it, I couldn't believe it was there. It was still so camouflaged. It was like a scene out of the book Tuck Everlasting. *There was the small freshwater stream, with a large fallen log to walk over it.*

To get inside the cabin you had to open an old fashioned Dutch door that was thick and heavy and "bear proof." Inside the cabin on one wall there are some knickknacks. One of those knickknacks on the shelf was designed by Mike and I, a wooden chessboard. . . complete with and myself carved wooden pieces out of two types of wood.

It's no resort cabin, this thing was hand built by some young guys years ago with a dream in their heads. I've been back a couple of times. On one of those occasions we participated in the Wilderness Pentathlon. That year I came in with some of the best times. . .but I lost due to the age handicap system to Sandy's nearly 80-year-old father, Mac. It was one of the best times I've ever had with one of the greatest traditions I've ever heard of.

I want to go back one day. I hope it remains there, untouched, unbothered, and rustic as you can possibly imagine.

Wade

February 20, 2016
This was my second trip up and it will likely be my last for spell. We're moving from Oregon next month and I feel like this [cabin] was one of the friends I needed to say goodbye to before I left.

This place is a gem unlike any other. The stories are literally baked into the cabin itself. . . .The lake was snowy and slightly frozen in the middle. I got a skiff of snow this morning. [the] cabin is in great shape.

R, I left you a neck knife hanging on the west wall. It's yours if you want. I figure if you ever can't find the cabin and [are forced to] spend the night [out in the elements] again, it could be useful."

Ben

✦

I hiked to the cabin in the snow, once. It was never a dream of mine to experience a February trip to the cabin, let alone a trip over Valentines weekend with my Dad, sister and Uncle Rob. Not that they weren't the best Valentines a girl could ask for, but because I was emoting in the way that only a single twenty-something on Valentines can.

Nursing a broken heart, I went up to forget and freeze a little. I hoped to get back to nature and hopefully some of that cold Oregon wintertime could ease the ache. However, this trip would be better than I could have expected and even more than I needed to regain normalcy and move on with life.

Only a few things stand out to me now. Without pictures I have a hard time remembering anything anymore. It was cold and some of the prettiest trail I can remember. The nearly 5-mile hike to the cabin has always been full of wonders. I always saw something new. One of my favorite parts was hiking along a clearing on the literal side of the mountain. Just rocks glimmering in the sun covered in soft green moss. But this time, it was just snow. Snow always makes things beautiful, but it turned the hike up to the cabin into a magically quiet world. It seemed we were much more away from society than normal.

I remember someone, probably Dad, had the idea to build an igloo. At the time, I was not too interested but wanted to help anyway. Emily was a much better sidekick than I and helped the most. However, not being the best assistant hasn't stopped me from bragging to my children that of course I have built an igloo and I am the greatest adventurer they know.

The igloo was a labor of love. Emily and Dad slept in it that night. Regretfully, I opted to sleep in the cabin. I think the igloo was warmer.

Being cold, we didn't get to do our normal cabin activities. No swim in Sally Lake. No dozing by the stream watching little frog's play and jump. But, it still seemed that before I was ready, it was time to go. The hike down seemed more treacherous than normal, and it probably was with all that snow.

My dad and Uncle Rob know the trail to the cabin so well they could get there in the middle of the night without a flashlight. In fact, they probably have. This makes them the best guides up and down the mountain; especially when there are snow making markers, and sometimes the trail itself, disappear.

I must have been having a slow time getting down the mountain, because at one point my Uncle Rob told me that it would be much faster to just slide down the hill. I mean what's the point of feet anyway when you have a nice round bum for a sled? I was hesitant to say the least, but he knew me well enough that if he went down, the peer pressure would be too great and I would not be willing to chicken out.

He handed me one of his hiking poles, and taking the other prepared to slide down the hill. Sitting down, he secured his heels in the snow and leaned back against his hiking pole to be used as a guide. I'm sure he said something amazing and worthy of repeating here, but I can't remember. It was probably a Jeremiah Johnson quote. Then down he went, easy as pie to the trail below. It was only maybe only 50 yards, if that far. If that 'old man' could do it, I thought, what was stopping me?

My trepidation gone, I readied myself. Just like my Uncle Rob, feet planted and hiking pole to guide me, I started to slide. Faster and faster I went down. I'm pulled away from the rush of the slide when I feel a stinging pain in my right hand. It was ungloved and the beautiful soft snow began feeling like cold glass shards on my exposed skin.

Instinctively, I lifted my hand up, releasing the pressure from the pole and taking me faster and faster down the snowy hill. I start to reel inside my head as my body started turning this way and that, the hill taking me wherever it wants. Then, out of nowhere, there was a stick.

Now for reference, you could imagine the top three feet of a tree, just sticking out of the snow. This stick was sturdy. It wasn't going anywhere, but I was. Faster and faster I flew, but as soon as I saw that stick, I froze. I became one with that snowy hill and the hill knew it. No longer was I sliding back and forth, but headed straight for the stick. I lost my mind. I wanted to protect myself (mostly my face) and not wanting to release the pole again, I lifted my legs to block my body.

The stick grabbed my right (upper) thigh and threw me backwards. It might have even threw me in the air a little. Then it was over. There I was, laying on the trail, looking up at my family.

I don't remember their reaction. I hope they laughed. I hope I laughed.

I'm really glad I was still able to have children.

I love the cabin. I am eagerly awaiting the time I can take my kids up. I have three that could make it easily now. I can't wait for them to experience the joys I had there. I am grateful for the s acrifice that was made to build it. It is something I hold sacred and dear.

But a word of caution: Wear gloves if it's snowy. And definitely try sledding down the trail.

Desirae

🛨

January 2002
"Just dreaming. . . Most of the Douglas fir trees in the area are dying from some insect. Seems a shame to see them go to waste. Always wanted a Viking log house. Snow flurries with sun.

Solo trip to see the snow. Not much snow until halfway up the trail, but not disappointed after that: one foot [deep] by the lunch tree, two feet by the slide, three feet by the corner, and four feet by the berry patch. Three-plus feet at the cabin by Saturday PM, increased almost another foot by Sunday a.m. [It was almost] level with the window out back, and about six inches from the eve out front, due to [snow sliding off the cabin roof.] Snowshoes work well in the trees; but [I] sink in over my knees even with the snowshoes in the open areas. No tracks on the trail.

The toilet seat was an experience [to sit on, since it had] a thin layer of clear ice bonded to the seat.

The trees are laden with snow; many look like spears with their white and limbs press down vertically, almost touching the trunks. The creek is running strong. Along both sides are vertical snow banks, three to five feet high. The faces of the snow banks are scored by countless small snow slides, giving the whole thing the appearance of an exotic other worldly canyon in miniature.

Occasional gusts of wind will create large snowfalls from over-laden tree limbs, which results in mini blizzards below, sometimes for a distance of 100 yards or so away from the source tree. I recommend boots with the gaiters for this kind of snow and a light rain shell [jacket] with hood. Pushing through the branches, the regular dumping of snow down the back of my neck did keep me awake. It was refreshing, but I'll wear a hood next time.

It's incredibly quiet here now except for the murmur of the creek, the forest is wrapped in silence. Saw one furtive little bird and one large mouse, but that is all. Used to see snowshoe hares many years ago.

Surprisingly, in such silence (or maybe because of it), the life force of the Forest seems particularly intense. The trees are quiescent, but I sense them yearning for the return of spring to renew their battle with the elements and with one another. The living energy of the woods it is almost palpable beneath my feet, flowing through the roots and burrows, to the very earth itself; straining against the oppression of eternity and inviting us to put aside our foolish pursuits and revel in the joy of livingness.

The cabin has almost four feet of heavy snow on the roof. It groaned and creaked all night. I swept off the porch roof and about halfway up the front side; left the rest—it's too much work. The cabin is toasty warm and I'm watching the icicles grow on the eves as I write. Well it's about time to finish the peaches and head back down [to civilization]; after one more shot of Old Ezra's."

   Rob

Chapter 10
12. Part of the words in this sentence came from the initial dialog from the beginning of the movie Jeremiah Johnson, 1972

Acknowledgments

Duringthe creation of this book I relied heavily on the help of others. Before anyone else is mentioned, I must first thank my wife, Sandy, who has been totally supportive and encouraging throughout this entire process. She has played several roles during the writing of this book: spouse, friend, critic, fan, editor, book title creator, even my therapist. This book would not have ever been written without her, or even exist without her. We did this together.

Rachel has been my invaluable professional book editor and ghostwriter. Without her brilliant efforts working behind-the-scenes, my story would not exist. She has helped make this book become a reality. Her commitment to this entire project has been unwavering. She is such a good person. She is wise beyond her years. Her love of adventure, and especially the great outdoors, brought a wealth of passion and enthusiasm toward having my story being told the way it has. It was no miracle we were introduced; rather, it was Providence that brought Rachel into my world.

Thanks to Aaron Snethen for creating the book interior design. Also thanks to Taylor Piva for her excellent final proofing of the book.

Bobby Kuber's cover design is amazing. He took an actual picture of "The Big Cedar Tree" and made the front of the book come alive and in my mind "invite" all readers to discover for themselves what is "By The Big Cedar Tree." Working with Kuber Media Group opened my eyes to the world of becoming an author and I especially want Bobby to know that I'm appreciative of all his behind the scenes publishing and media work.

About the Author

John Embury was born in Salem, Oregon. In his youth, hiking became John's pathway to the world of nature and discovery—a pathway that has continued throughout his entire life.

His high school accomplishments in Track and Field opened the door for John to attend college on an athletic scholarship. Eventually, he earned his Bachelor of Arts degree from George Fox University and has worked in the health insurance and pharmaceutical industries for almost forty years.

He is a father of five children: A son and four beautiful daughters. After thirty-six years of marriage to Sandy, they now have three sons-in-law and six grandchildren. He and Sandy have lived in Boise, Idaho, since 1992. By his own definition, John is just an ordinary guy who values his family and friendships above all else. By The Big Cedar Tree is his first book.

CPSIA information can be obtained
at www.ICGtesting.com
Printed in the USA
FSHW021721091019
62789FS